Getting School-Wise

A Student Guidebook

Carol A. Josel

A SCARECROWEDUCATION BOOK

The Scarecrow Press, Inc.
Lanham, Maryland, and London
2002

A SCARECROWEDUCATION BOOK

Published in the United States of America
by Scarecrow Press, Inc.
A Member of the Rowman & Littlefield Publishing Group
4720 Boston Way
Lanham, Maryland 20706
www.scarecroweducation.com

ISBN 0-8108-4194-0

∞™ The paper used in this publication meets the minimum requirements of
American National Standard for Information Sciences—Permanence of
Paper for Printed Library Materials, ANSI/NISO Z39.48-1992.
Manufactured in the United States of America.

To my daughter, Gavrielle, and in memory of my dear Alan

Contents

Part 4: Learning Style Activities

Part 5: Note-Taking Activities

Part 6: Study Skill Activities

Regardless of age, status, or ability, most children share a common need for academic coping skills, which is the aim and focus of *Getting School-Wise*. From beginning to end, it serves as a guide to management and learning strategies that lead to school success and can either be used in its entirety or for targeting specific strategy needs.

Introductory activities are followed by organization and homework suggestions, while the next section disproves the common complaint that there's never enough time and offers numerous remedies for structuring time more efficiently. The learning styles unit then follows, fostering awareness and encouraging students to enhance their ability to process and access information by borrowing from their nondominant modalities.

Meanwhile, in classrooms everywhere, students struggle to record every spoken word, interrupting for repeats, sometimes even giving up, and so note-taking solutions are provided next. Teachers' signals of importance, usually imparted by tone, phrasing, and/or body language, are presented, as is the essential skill of abbreviating. Because covering a topic in class is only the beginning, Francis Robinson's SQ3R is included to promote students' ownership of material under study. They follow its steps, surveying and developing questions in a two-column format so that they can then respond and review out loud. These notes become instant study guides. Moreover, since memory aids improve learning, the next unit begins with fascinating "brainy" facts and covers everything from creating acronyms and sentence cues to visualization techniques. Brain teasers follow for a mental workout.

The final section offers strategies for successful test taking. Being well prepared is the key, but confidence is enhanced by knowing how to tackle true/false, matching, and multiple-choice questions while recognizing embedded clues. Included are essay tests, where it's not just a matter of spotting the right answer but being able to recall the information and organize it into a well-written response. All such test-taking needs are covered here, even practice writing leads.

Thus focused on time management, learning, and test-taking strategies, *Getting School-Wise* provides classroom-tested activities designed to enhance students' ability to achieve their academic goals and gain independence, while providing teachers with the tools to help make that happen.

Part I: Introductory Activities

A. Board Quotes

"There is an island of hope in the middle of every difficulty." ~ Successories

"You'll always miss 100 percent of the shots you don't take." ~ Successories

"The power to shape the future is earned through persistence. No other quality is as essential to success. . . . It is the ability to move mountains one grain of sand at a time." ~ Successories

"If better is possible, then good is not good enough." ~ unknown

"You are capable, competent, creative, and careful. Now prove it!" ~ Amanda Calzo's mom

"If you're not the lead dog, the view never changes." ~ Alex George's dad

"If we expect children to do well, they will." ~ Maureen Stout

"Education is the biggest gift you'll get from me—and you'll need it!" ~ Josiah Tam's mom

"Parents can only give good advice or put [children] on the right paths, but the final forming of a person's character lies in his own hands." ~ Anne Frank

"Home is the place where, when you have to go there, they have to take you in." ~ Robert Frost

"Just because something is difficult doesn't mean you shouldn't try. It means you should try harder." ~ Argus

"For every person who climbs the ladder of success, there are a dozen waiting for the elevator." ~ Successories

"You make your choices, and your choices make you." ~ Steve Beckman's dad

"Remember how you felt when you heard particularly good news. Then walk and stand like that." ~ Barbara Asher

"Don't accept 'good enough' as good enough." ~ unknown

"For all the sad words of tongue or pen, the saddest of these: 'It might have been.'" ~ John Greenleaf Whittier

"Education is a gift that is given to us, and, if we accept it, we will turn wise." ~ Enrique Torres

"Men . . . derive their conviction of their own possibilities largely from the estimate formed of them by others." ~ Frederick Douglass

"If the old will remember, the very young will listen."~ Chief Dan George

"To forget one's ancestors is to be a brook without a source, a tree without roots." ~ Chinese Proverb

"Books are uniquely portable magic." ~ Stephen King

"A book is like a garden carried in the pocket." ~ Chinese Proverb

"A book shut tight is but a block of paper." ~ unknown

"Books help readers see beyond the edges of their own experience." ~ Judith Hendershot

B. The Changeling Eagle

1. So what's the point? That's what you want your students to discover, so stress that before reading this Native American tale to them. Once students have jotted down their opinions about the story's message, group them into triads and ask each to come to consensus. Whole class sharing and discussion then follow.

2. As you discuss "expectations," and how we rise or fall to meet them, consider sharing with your students a study I learned about years ago from a college professor: about fifty children, all with similar socio-economic backgrounds, intelligence, and age were divided into two classes, with teachers of similar backgrounds, ages, and experience. Teacher A was advised that she would be hard-pressed to kccp up with her high-caliber students. Teacher B, on the other hand, was warned about the low-level students awaiting her. The results prove the point. Teacher A found that her students were so bright, so thirsty for learning, that she was spending hours every day preparing for them and had a hard time staying ahead of them. Teacher B got just what she expected, too. Her students were reluctant to do any work, barely passed her tests, and seemed quite uninterested in any of her lessons!

3. This is also a good time to talk about popular stereotypes, many all-too familiar to your students. Just mention such words as *preppies, geeks, teenagers, teachers, college students*, etc. and you'll get an earful. Case in point: 1992's Teen Talk Barbie who squealed, "Math class is tough." Choose one or two stereotypes and have your students jot down as many applicable adjectives. Record these on the board, putting a plus or minus sign next to each, as you talk about the effects such beliefs have on behavior, sense of self-worth, acceptance, etc. Sharon Begley, in her article, "The Stereotype Trap," wrote, "There is a growing body of evidence that suggests stereotypes strongly influence self-perception and have startling implications for many students. Stanford University psychologist, Claude Steele's research found that stereotypes such as 'ditzy blondes,' make people painfully aware of how society views them—so painfully aware that knowledge of the stereotype can affect how well they do on intellectual and other tasks." (*Newsweek,* November 6, 2000). Just think about the educational labels we attach to children and the accompanying expectations they generate. Food for thought and discussion.

C. Me and My Folks

1. Ask such questions as:

    Ever quarreled with a parent?
    Always do as you are told?
    Ever visit museums, the movies, plays with your parents?
    How many times per week family has dinner together?
    Have a parent(s) who asks about the school day?
    Ever ask about mom/dad's day?

2. Have students share family traditions and rituals, maybe steak for Thanksgiving and gift opening on Christmas Eve? Can be done as a journal entry.

3. Ask students to complete "Me and My Folks," then poll each item and share.

4. Compare the advantages and disadvantages of buying/bringing lunch and find out their usual fare. Most kids eat way too much fat, sodium, and sugar! Did you know that a typical can of soda contains between seven and nine teaspoons of sugar—even ginger ale?

5. Have students complete the "Me and My Folks, Part II" T-Chart, starring what they consider the most important improvements they need to make and discuss.

6. Related to the idea of families and traditions, etc. is the realization that we must actively seek out the stories of our parents, grandparents, and, if lucky, even great-grandparents, before it is too late. Valuing personal histories enriches lives, and this is a perfect opportunity to encourage students to interview and tape/videotape the ensuing conversations. I have my dad on videotape, a gift my daughter can then offer to her children, and so on.

Part 2: Organization and Homework Activities

A. Board Quotes

"Success is never final." ~ unknown

"Commitment is a line you cross. It's the difference between wishing and doing." ~ Successories

"On the road to success, you can be sure of one thing. . . . There is never a crowd on the extra mile." ~ unknown

"The difference between a successful person and others is not a lack of knowledge but attitude." ~ Successories

"You never fail until you stop trying." ~ Josiah Tam

Many times the difference between success and failure is doing something nearly right . . . or doing it exactly right." ~ Successories

"Success is measured by effort." ~ unknown

"The fact that you'll never reach perfection is no excuse for aiming at less." ~ unknown

"For every person who climbs the ladder of success, there are a dozen waiting for the elevator." ~ Successories

"Homework builds the skills needed to cope with life." ~ Linda Sanna

"Homework extends the learning process beyond the four walls of the classroom, and reinforces the process by giving children a chance to practice skills covered at school." ~ Linda Sanna

"If you're not sure of where you're going, you're likely to end up somewhere else." ~ unknown

"Excellence is the result of caring more than others think is wise, risking more than others think is safe, dreaming more than is practical, and expecting more than others think is possible." ~ Successories

"If you always do what you've always done, you'll always get what you've always gotten." ~ unknown

"A goal without a plan is a dream." ~ anonymous

"The ability to block out the unnecessary puts the goal within reach." ~ Successories

"If one advances confidently in the direction of his dreams and endeavors to live the life which he has imagined, he will meet with success." ~ Henry David Thoreau

"It's easier to go down the mountain than up, but the view is always best from the top." ~ Successories

"Determine to pay the price of a worthy goal. The trials you encounter will introduce you to your strengths." ~ Epictetus, Roman teacher & philosopher

"You become successful once you start moving toward a worthwhile goal." ~ Successories

"In life, reach for the stars. What's in between is just empty space." ~ Barbara Morrison's dad

"Reach for the moon; if you fall short, you may land on a star." ~ unknown

"You can't build a reputation on what you're going to do." ~ Henry Ford

B. Actually

1. Have students complete the True/False questions on their own, as you read the items to them. Then poll student responses as noted on the bottom of the page.

2. Discuss each item, offering simple solutions/explanations as you go along, including:

   - All the problems associated with cramming and leaving things to the last minute. Have they ever forgotten something during a test they studied so well for the night before? Have they ever received a low grade because of a hastily put together project or writing assignment? They'll know exactly what you're talking about!
   - My mother's mantra: If you take it out, put it back in the same place.
   - The probability that if it's not written down, it will be forgotten, stressing the necessity of recording all assignments and the advantages of to-do lists.
   - Provide a monthly calendar to each student for the purpose of recording upcoming assignments and tests, as well as long-term projects, reports, etc. (See appendix)
   - The advisability of keeping all school supplies in one place to avoid wasting time searching.
   - The importance of sorting through notebooks, if not nightly, then weekly. Keep a supply of dividers and notebook paper reinforcements on hand in the classroom. A hole punch, too.
   - The importance of storing completed units of study at home in either a box, large-ringed notebook, or file drawer. Remind students that teachers occasionally mis-record grades and always have the option of administering a final exam. Work should also be held onto because it is valued—not tossed in the nearest trashcan!
   - The usefulness of homework folders. Provide or require that students purchase a two-pocket (Duotang) folder. Punch holes in them for storage in notebooks. These then become homework folders, with new handouts stored on one side each day and transferred to the other pocket upon completion. This eliminates the refrain, "I did it but can't find it!" Once graded and returned, assignments should be stored in the appropriate Homework section of the notebook.

C. Tips on Getting Organized

1. Ask your students to consider their kitchens, where and how things are stored. Is mom always hunting for the canned peas, or does she know right where they are? Personally, my spices are lined up in alphabetical order and my canned goods are stacked by category! And how about their bedrooms? Any hunting going on, especially during the morning rush? And what about you, your organizing strategies or shortcomings?

2. Next ask students to check off the suggestions *not* currently being done on the Tips page. This activity reinforces many of the ideas already presented, with just a few exceptions:

   - Establishing a time-line for long-term assignments, something a number of children may require assistance with.

- Carrying a separate, medium-sized, different-colored notebook for each subject. This works well for most but not all students. Some claim it is too unwieldy, etc. In that case, insist on a large binder with a separate section for each subject. Those sections, in turn, need dividers for notes, quizzes/tests, and homework. Pencil cases are also advised. Some children will need your help organizing their notebooks initially—many periodically thereafter, too. Meanwhile, involve parents, encouraging them to make this a weekly home ritual.
- Encourage the use of a Drop Spot (p. 40), a place to gather all books, papers, etc. needed in school the next day.

3. Then direct students to complete and share their Organizing Plan. These should be revisited periodically.

D. Post Near Your Drop Spot

I have a Drop Spot where, each evening, I stack my book bag, lunch bag, keys, purse, etc. Before that, I was known to drive off in the morning with my purse hanging on a doorknob or lunch still in the fridge! This Drop Spot reminder can be duplicated on colored paper, laminated, and handed out. Students should place it in a suitable location for collecting school-related materials—preferably every evening before going to bed.

E. In a Box, Basket, Shelf, or Drawer

1. Ask students about where they do their schoolwork and how well supplied that space is. Is everything in easy reach or do they waste time hunting around the house for everything from pencils to paper clips?

2. Students should then check off their current supplies and record those they need to purchase.

F. School Life and You

1. Writer Barry Lane, in his *After the End: Teaching and Learning Creative Revision,* teaches the effectiveness of thoughtshots—"a look at what a character is thinking and feeling—in writing." Here you'll ask students for a thoughtshot—what's in their head—the moment you say, "There will be a *test* on this tomorrow." Right then and there, direct them to jot down their first thought. You can guess what they're thinking, can't you? Now try it with such words as *school* and *report cards*. Not only are thoughtshots an effective writing tool, you'll discover that they are a quick and certain means of getting to the heart of things. Can be done as a journal entry.

2. Ask your students to respond in writing to these two questions: a) What is the value of an education? b) What is your definition of a good student? (This makes a good journal entry). Later they should pose these questions to three people, preferably a parent, teacher, and friend. Responses can then be shared and discussed the next day.

3. Share Ogden Nash's "The Pretty Good Student" poem, asking students to then react to the ideas presented. Be sure to ask them if they would like to be taught by a pretty good teacher, treated by a pretty good physician, fly with a pretty good pilot, etc. (See appendix)

4. Ask students to define *self-confidence* and *motivation* and then discuss. Emphasize that self-confidence/esteem must be earned, that every work of art doesn't necessarily deserve a place on the fridge, and that every good deed needn't be rewarded with stickers, money, or what have you. Mention, too, such external sources of motivation as bribes, sports requirements, and parental approval. What really counts, though, are the internal motivators, such as self-satisfaction and the desire to keep improving—competing with one's self. Just consider the jogger who last year could barely make it around the block but today jogs for a couple of miles.

5. Now have your students check off those statements that hold true for them, while making note of those that need doing, turning the most important into promises at the bottom of the page.

6. As you address each suggestion, stress the work ethic, the desirability of active participation, the importance of asking questions—even at the risk of appearing "stupid"—learning from mistakes, doing one's best, accountability, making excuses, blaming others (especially teachers), the impact of school absence, frustration, the lessons of failing, and so on.

7. As a follow-up, read *The Little Engine That Could.*

G. Homework: Getting It Right!/Planning on It

1. Have students complete a T-Chart (see appendix), recording the benefits of homework on one side and the issues they have with it on the other. Can be done as a journal entry. Be sure to remind students that it is all but impossible to fail a course if all homework is completed and turned in.

2. Use these activities as an assessment to establish how your students tackle their schoolwork, expanding on each response. Be sure to stress the necessity of recording all assignments, tackling the hardest subject(s) first, the advisability of a daily schedule, taking short breaks between assignments, reviewing/studying out loud for tests, chunking large assignments into smaller, more manageable tasks, and the importance of reading, its impact on everything else, etc. (More on these topics throughout this book.) When I teach this, I am often reminded of Bill Bradley's quote, "I was determined that no one would outwork me." That just about says it all.

3. When this has been completed, "Planning On It" asks students to record those tips that are already being implemented, together with those they need to incorporate. These should be shared and revisited periodically.

4. For those students who find too many distractions in their bedrooms, suggest that they begin work at the kitchen table, in full view of a parent who can then intervene when signs of inattention or frustration surface. But only if it's quiet!

H. Phone Buddies

Talk about the problems associated with absences, all that is missed and how the world stops for no one. If sick, however, it is imperative that kids have a buddy or two who will step in and collect work for them—hopefully getting it to them as well. If that's impossible, work can be piled on the main office counter for a parent to pick up. Establish buddies in class.

I. Homework Helper Sites

Ask for additions to this list, keeping in mind that websites come and go. It's, therefore, advisable to check all of these beforehand.

J. Visions and Goals

1. First, ask everyone to record what they see as their jobs/responsibilities as students and share some of their views.

2. Then instruct students to go back through all their completed pages, starring or highlighting the most important improvements they plan to make and jotting down their top eight.

3. Now talk about the importance of goals and resolutions, how easy it is to lose sight of them, such as those made on New Year's Eve. What about the resolutions you've not kept over the years? Anything

like my traditional promises to lose weight, exercise daily, eat nutritiously, abandon bad habits, etc.? Share your successes and failures.

4. Finally, give everyone an opportunity to record five short-term goals they want to reach, to be revisited often.

Part 3: Time Management Activities

A. Board Quotes

"Ain't it funny how time slips away." ~ Willie Nelson

"I recommend that you learn to take care of the minutes, for the hours will take care of themselves." ~ Lord Chesterfield

"Time is but the stream I go fishing in." ~ Henry David Thoreau

"Hold every moment sacred." ~ Thomas Mann

"Time isn't your enemy until you kill it." ~ unknown

"People forget how fast you did a job—but they always remember how well you did it." ~ Howard W. Newton

"Procrastination is the killer of time and the graveyard of opportunity." ~ unknown

"Time is the most valuable thing a person can spend." ~ unknown

"Time is swift, it races by. Opportunities are born and die." ~ Winnie the Pooh

"This is the beginning of a new day. You have been given this day to use as you will. You can waste it or use it for good. What you do today is important because you are exchanging a day of your life for it. When tomorrow comes, this day will be gone forever; in its place is something that you've left behind. . . . Let it be something good." ~ Successories

"Finish each day and be done with it. You have done what you could. . . . Tomorrow is a new day; begin it well." ~ Ralph Waldo Emerson

"Those who spend time boasting about the wonderful things they will do tomorrow probably spent yesterday doing the same thing." ~ unknown

"Take time for all things." ~ Benjamin Franklin

"One thing is certain: When you spend money, it is possible to acquire more. Once you have spent time, it is gone forever. The lesson for all of us is, I suppose, to do the meaningful things while there is still time." ~ Greg Crosby

B. Where and When Should You Study? The Scoop on Where and When

1. First, ask if anyone has ever run out of time, never had enough time, said that time flies? Then, of course, the question becomes, what is time? Ask this of your students, having them: 1) Define *time*, without using *time* in their definition. This is not easy, but I promise that you'll receive a few gems, like the 8th grade definitions below; 2) Identify their favorite use of free time. (One 8th grader indicated that she spent most of her time staring at a boy's picture!); and 3) Rate their use of time on a scale from one to five, with one suggesting there's almost no accounting for time and five for your strict agenda types. Sharing can be quite illuminating! This can be done as a journal entry.

"It's something that's never on your side, but it gives you the motivation to succeed." ~ Anthony DiGinto

"Time is what keeps the universe alive. It's what enlightens and kills us. It's another thing that tells us we are mortal." ~ Damien Martin

"It's something that starts and ends so quickly, you don't even know where it went." ~ Walter Goraczko

"Time is the forward motion of life which can't, as we know it, be reversed." ~ Danny Astacio

"Time is a privilege." ~ Dan Cramer

2. Now ask the children to respond to the true/false items and then "score" themselves. Then go over each statement, expanding on the answers; explanations are provided on the next two pages. After discussing, scores can be shared by a show of hands, launching this unit.

C. Time Control: Getting to Know Sam

1. Before introducing this activity, ask for a show of hands on these questions:
   - School-morning wake-up call? 6:00, 6:30, 7:00 A.M. . . .
   - Breakfast eaters? Cereal, doughnut, bagel, egg, zip (Encourage a healthy breakfast as research suggests it promotes academic success.)
   - Length of ride to school? <15 minutes, 15–30 minutes, and so on.
   - Homework start-up time? For those after-dinner sorts, talk about waning energies and the effects of a long day and big meal. Anyone ever NOT finished homework because of exhaustion?
   - Snacking fare? Recall for students the sugar load of a can of soda with its 7 and 9 teaspoons, providing a brief sugar high followed by a rapid downward slide.
   - Time on task? <30 minutes, 30, 60, 90, . . . (Two hours a day for assignments, reviews, and test preps vastly improves performance).
   - Work environment? Quiet, background music, TV? (Encourage silence, as concentration requires much energy and channeling extra to tune out distracting sounds is twice as tiring!)
   - Parental role? Hands-on, keeping a watchful eye, test reviewer only, hands-off, other?
   - Daily reading? For homework? Pleasure? Bedtime ritual? (Improves everything!)
   - Bedtime? 9:00, 9:30, 10:00, 10:30 p.m. . . . Too tired to work? Get more sleep!

2. Examining Sam's schedule, have students jot down in their journals what's looking good and where improvements are called for. After sharing, remind students that by middle school, two hours of schoolwork per day is not unreasonable. Can they find two hours of work time for Sam who claims he's just too busy? Space is provided. Share; discuss.

D. Your Own Schedule

Using Sam's schedule as a model, have students complete their own *typical* weekday schedule, and then highlight/star times when more work time could be included without compromising down time. Some students may already be stretched pretty thin with after-school activities and responsibilities. They will have to be a bit more creative in carving out their two hours—perhaps even rising 30 minutes earlier to finish up.

E. The Weekend Is Here!

1. Remind children that, for most, sleeping habits change on the weekend and should be taken into account.

2. Some students use weekends to good advantage, working on projects, taking text notes, reviewing, and catching up. Others need convincing. Adult errands and household tasks don't grind to a halt

come Friday evening. . . . When completed, ask students to go back and find time slots for school-work. Time and responsibilities don't stop just because we have the day off!

F. Sam's 168

1. Stress the 168 hours-a-week fact and the reality that there are no dress rehearsals, often only regrets. Talk, too, about choices and how doing nothing is a choice in itself, affecting plans, dreams, how we conduct the business of our lives.

2. Before examining Sam's 168, explain that time is segmented into decimals instead of fractions or whole numbers to simplify calculations. On the board, write:

   .25 = 15 minutes (¼ hour)
   .50 = 30 minutes (½ hour)
   .75 = 45 minutes (¾ hour)
   1.00 = 60 minutes (one hour)

3. Recalling Sam's claim to be so busy that dedicating any additional time to schoolwork is out of the question, ask students to examine his 168, carefully noting how he apportions his time. Go over each category to avoid confusion, explaining, for example, that school travel is in two directions, five times a week; meals are usually eaten three times a day, seven days a week, and so on. Then note the total hours expended before focusing on the unaccounted-for ones. All 42½ of them! He's awake but. . . . This sets the stage for students to calculate their own time use.

G. Your 168

1. Reminding students to use decimals and round off to the nearest quarter in their time calculations, monitor them as they itemize, add, and multiply, checking for accuracy.

2. Now comes the fun part. After children total their hours per day and per week, have them do some subtracting to come up with their own unaccounted-for hours.

3. As each student shares his total unaccounted-for hours per week, record the numbers on the board. All those hours will serve as quite an eye opener, promising a lot of "retooling!" No one in your class will ever be able to say to you, "I didn't have enough time!"

H. Timely Tips

Having now assessed their use of time, it's time to make some changes, some new choices. As you go over each tip offered in this follow-up activity, invite students to respond with Sometimes (S), Always (A), or Never (N). Encourage list making by sharing one of your own, if you're dependent on them, and provide index cards for daily task noting—and, of course, crossing off!

I. Count 'Em Up!

Once scoring has been completed and shared, ask students to note the timely improvements they intend to put into action right away—and hold them to it!

J. Daily Schedule

Photocopy this schedule on both sides and offer every other week. This will help keep kids task-oriented and on target, tackling hardest subjects first, accommodating breaks and favorite programming, and heading for bed—book in hand—at a reasonable hour each night.

Part 4: Learning Style Activities

A. Board Quotes

"Every person that you meet knows something you don't; learn from them." ~ unknown

"A man's mind, stretched by a new idea, can never go back to its original dimensions." ~ Oliver Wendell Holmes

"Tell me, I forget. Show me, I remember. Involve me, I understand." ~ Ancient Chinese Proverb

"People don't all learn the same way. And to improve your study skills, you need to understand how you learn best." ~ *Philadelphia Inquirer* (9/25/98)

"You are your most valuable asset. Don't forget that. You are the best thing you have." ~ Gary Paulsen (*Hatchet*)

"Our life would be what we made of it—nothing more, nothing less." ~ Paul Zindel (*Pigman*)

"The brain does a better job retaining information connected with rhythm and rhyme." ~ Pat Wolfe

"You did what you knew how to do, and when you knew better, you did better." ~ Maya Angelou

"We learn . . . 10% of what we read, 20% of what we hear, 30% of what we see, 50% of what we both see and hear, 70% of what is discussed with others, 80% of what we experience personally, and 95% of what we teach to someone else." ~ William Glasser (see appendix)

"We tend to like what we do well and do well that which we like." ~ unknown

B. Finding the F's

As they say, the mind works in wondrous ways, and here is a fun and intriguing way to prove the point. We simply all see things differently, irrespective of intelligence. It is, therefore, highly unlikely that all of your students will immediately identify all seven F's in this short paragraph. When this activity was first presented to me at a hemisphericity workshop, I identified only three. The woman seated beside me insisted there were six. And even after being told there were seven, I still saw only three! Use this activity to launch your unit on learning styles—how we all "see" things differently, tackle tasks differently. Enjoy!

C. Finding Yourself: The Visual, Auditory, and Kinesthetic Learner

It's time for your students to assess how they best take in and process information. Most will probably discover that one of their senses dominates, while others may find that they rely on all three fairly equally.

Ask students to complete all three assessments, checking off those statements that most apply to them and then recording their "score." Once done, take a poll to discover the types of learners seated before you. This information will be useful as you plan your daily lessons. Most of us use a combination of modalities but rely more heavily on one. Effective teaching takes into account all three learning styles.

D. Sharpening That Learning Style

1. There is, of course, always room for improvement and here that comes in the form of enhancing our dominant modality and borrowing strategies from the other two, thus complementing our own.

a. Ask students which type of learner might expect to find school more difficult. The answer is the kinesthetic learner, the one who needs, more than the others, to move about and manipulate their world in order to learn. The typical classroom affords few such opportunities, with the exception of science labs and the expressive arts. Remind everyone, however, that a very effective way for all to learn is to put their bodies into it—rehearsing information out loud to a clapped beat, a rhythmic march.

b. Students should now highlight strategies from all three modalities to bolster their own learning style and reinforce what they are already doing. To that end, go over each item, explaining and demonstrating some, such as the structural analysis of words, the use of graphic organizers (see appendix for samples), mnemonics, repetition, flash cards (see memory unit), the power of rhythm and music as in the alphabet song, pacing and walking while learning, physical reenactments of narratives, as in history lessons, and highlighting to maintain focus. Try giving your students a list of ten items to learn quickly, quiz them, and ask how they tackled this task.

2. Again, think about your own learning style, which, in turn, dictates your teaching style and try to include activities that will involve all learners. The easiest way to do this is by providing choices. For instance, you might allow children to work alone, with a partner or in a small group. Sometimes you might allow students to write, draw, or enact a scene from a story or content area topic. And, so as not to overwhelm your more reluctant readers, try spreading out reading assignments over a period of days, such as assigning one section at a time, rather than the entire chapter. You might also offer books on tape, along with your regular lending library.

3. For your visual learners:

- Put vocabulary, important facts, homework on the board or overhead.
- Remind students to carefully look at textbook graphics and their accompanying captions.
- Repeat oral instructions and, if possible, put these on the board as well.
- Provide and/or have students create graphic organizers.
- Cluster information on the board during lectures and discussions.

For your auditory learners:

- Read introductions and chapter summaries to the class.
- For more needy students, ask a volunteer to tape chapters, novels.
- Ask students to read end-of-chapter questions out loud prior to their reading of a chapter.
- Include whole class and small group discussions in your lessons.
- Read test and writing assignment directions out loud.
- Moving quickly from student to student, do a story retelling.
- Provide opportunities for oral presentations.

For your kinesthetic learners:

- Insist that notes be taken, helping focus attention on the material at hand and triggering the learning process.
- Encourage students to add pictures to definitions of unfamiliar vocabulary.
- Allow students to act out concepts, new vocabulary, etc. in small groups.
- Ask students to record new terms/definitions and dates/events on flash cards.
- Teach your poorer spellers to correctly write out difficult words across a long strip of paper and then repeatedly trace it with a finger as they say the word slowly, out loud. When confident, they can then self-test and check, repeating the process until they "own" the word. (VAKT)
- Have students turn stories/concepts/events into scripts for dramatizing.
- Set new learning to song, as was done early on with the alphabet song.

E. Where and How You Work

Now it's time to consider environmental learning styles, so, as you read these items, have your students circle their choices. Be sure to talk about your own ideal learning environment. Too warm, and I'll nap; too cold, and I'll focus on that and nothing else. And, for me, beds are for sleeping, the floor for exercising on or cleaning!

F. My Working Profile

1. Choosing from the word bank at the bottom of this page, have students fill in the blanks. These can then be displayed. Be sure to encourage them, regardless of preferences, to tackle homework as soon as possible after arriving home, to eat healthy snacks—not salt and sugar-laden ones, to study alone and out loud for tests before asking a friend or parent to quiz them.

2. There are a number of websites dedicated to learning styles, with some offering inventories your students can take to further assess their true learning style, such as www2.nc.edu/virtcol/ss/learn.html.

3. Some books to consider, as well: *Teaching Elementary Students Through Their Individual Learning Styles: Practical Approaches for Grades 3–6* by Rita Dunn and Kenneth Dunn, and *Teaching Secondary Students Through Their Individual Learning Styles: Practical Approaches for Grades 7–12* by Rita Dunn and Kenneth Dunn.

Part 5: Note-Taking Activities

A. Board Quotes

"Careful reading and good notes are essential to earning good grades consistently." ~ Ron Gray

"Students who take notes on their reading assignments perform better on exams." ~ Burke H. Bretzing

"When taking notes, students actively attend to ideas being studied, relate it to their own knowledge . . . and process the content more deeply." ~ Patricia L. Smith

"Two-column textbook and lecture notes provide study guides for easy review and recitation." ~ Carol Josel

"He listens well who takes notes." ~ Dante

"Graduates were exposed in the year 2000 to more information than their grandparents were in a lifetime." ~ Dr. Terrence Canning

B. What Was That You Just Said???

1. Going back to Barry Lane's thoughtshots, this activity asks students to honestly address their feelings about taking notes, everything from uncertainty as to what's important to record to losing focus, giving up, and writer's cramp. After they have jotted down at least five issues, ask for volunteers and record their comments on the board all around the word *note-taking*.

2. Then ask students to answer the five questions that follow, sharing and explaining their responses. In this way, most note-taking issues will be addressed. I have found that many students are very protective of their notes—sometimes lost by the borrower or returned too late to be of much use—and sensitive to their peers' criticism regarding such things as their handwriting, spelling errors, incompleteness, etc. Advise students that, if they follow the note-taking prescriptions set forth in this unit, their notes will most likely be so well abbreviated as to be unborrowable!

C. A New Way of Looking at Things

These abbreviated instructions for writing a business letter launch the lessons on abbreviated note-taking. This exercise is meant only as an introduction and is not meant to frustrate anyone so be sure to emphasize that fact, encouraging students to simply do their best to decipher these notes. Have them share their "translations," explaining that the full text follows on the next page.

D. So That's What It Said!

After your students have checked their work against the actual instructions, ask them to rate their results and take a poll. Then find out which abbreviations posed the fewest and most problems. Be sure to emphasize the need for patience. This takes time to master; we're just beginning!

E. Did You Know That You Should . . .

1. As a trial and to give your students a quick assessment of their note-taking ability, you many want to offer these tips as a lecture, providing a separate sheet of paper for their notes. Pace yourself as naturally as possible, expounding on certain items, while keeping an eye on their progress. If anyone asks for a repeat, refuse, and carry on. Afterward they can check their results with the original and highlight those they need to keep in mind.

    If you prefer, however, simply go over each item, expanding on them as you go along and instructing students to highlight those of particular significance for them

2. As for the Signals of Importance, be sure to dramatize each one as you go, waving arms, pausing, etc.

F. Note-Taking Shortcuts

1. The importance of good notes cannot be emphasized enough. Focus, then, on the fact that our memories inevitably fail us if information is not written down. Personally, I rarely make it through a grocery store with everything I need to purchase without my shopping list firmly in hand.

2. Now come the shortcuts: Some of these will be instant hits with your students, others are an acquired taste, while still others may very well be abandoned. The key to it all, though, is patience, practice, and developing their personal shorthand.

    Put several examples on the board and then let your students come up with some abbreviated sentences of their own for classmates to decipher.

    a. Eliminating some vowels:
        Jnny cn't ply 2day.
        Cndls cn be dngrus.
        Sme pepl say ruls shud be brkn.

    b. Eliminating unnecessary words:
        Dn't chnge ruls in mid of gme.
        Help is on way.

    c. Substituting = for verbs, especially linking verbs:
        Hiway = shortest rte thru cty.
        Smking = bad 4 u.
        L.room pics = prtty.

    d. Word beginnings: (see page 78)
        Mth = hrd 4 me.
        Sup. Ct. = hiest ct. in lnd.

e. Eliminating periods.

f. Coding placed in margin(s):
   Try *ionosphere, Beethoven, hypothesis*

g. Abbreviating:
   More to follow on page 79. For now, explain the two arrows and b/c:

   I'm going → mall b/c need 2 gfts; I'll leave ← hme.

G. Let's Practice

1. Point out the coded Beauregard = B and the use of arrows representing the words *to* and *from*.

2. Instruct students to quickly glance through the shortcuts on the previous page, making sure there is no confusion about any one item.

3. "Translate" the first sentence together for further clarification. The rest should be done independently, with you monitoring and assisting, as needed.

4. Once completed, have students self-check, followed by sharing and discussion.

H. Keep Practicing/Keep Going

1. First, give students a moment to rate their work on the previous page and share.

2. Again, remind students about the arrows, adding the abbreviation *w/* for *with*.

3. Then let students try their hand "decoding" these textbook terms, lending assistance, as needed.

4. Once completed and self-checked, discussion should follow and any problems shared.

I. Now, Get Those Abbs Working!

This list represents barely the tip of the iceberg when it comes to abbreviating words by relying on the first syllable, etc. Have students highlight any that might be unfamiliar and then brainstorm a whole new list together. Don't forget to include content area terms.

J. Another Kind of Abb Workout

1. These represent just a few of the symbols your students can practice incorporating into their notes. Again, have them highlight those they are unfamiliar with but particularly like. Then brainstorm more such symbols and add them to the list.

2. Explain that some people also abbreviate with an occasional graphic, such as a drawn heart to represent love, etc. This is fine as long as the pictures don't take longer than recording the words themselves!

K. Exercising All Those Abbs/Keep Going/Check It Out

1. The tables are now turned, and it's your students' turn to do the abbreviating. Remind them to flip through the previous pages for ideas, with you monitoring their efforts.

2. Once done, have volunteers write their renditions on the board, comparing these with those of classmates and my suggestions on the "Check It Out" page. Discussion should follow, as they grade their efforts and jot down their strengths and weaknesses.

L. Abbreviate! Abbreviate!

Instead of more unrelated sentences, here students are given practice abbreviating a passage based on the Battle of Bunker Hill. Provide paper and/or overhead transparencies for easier sharing. Again, remind everyone to refer back to previous pages and monitor their progress.

M. One Way of Looking at It

This page presents the Battle of Bunker Hill passage from the previous page in very abbreviated form. As students compare this version with their own, discuss the differences, what doesn't make sense, etc. It may likely seem extreme, but it's essential that students see the possibilities, as they develop their own personal shorthand. The key is practice.

N. Your Turn

1. In this final activity, instruct students to select a short textbook passage to carefully abbreviate and then exchange with a classmate for "translating." If desired, students can then "grade" each other's work. Text title and page must be included.

Part 6: Study Skill Activities

A. Board Quotes

"If you care enough about a result, you will most certainly attain it." ~ William James

"If you can do a job a little better each day, you'll one day find that you can do it better than anybody else." ~ unknown

"If you're coasting, you're going downhill." ~ J. T. Scully's dad

"If you always do what you've always done, you'll always get what you've always gotten." ~ Argus

"Don't just do enough to get by; do enough to get ahead." ~ Argus

"The difference between a successful person and others is not a lack of knowledge but rather of will." ~ Successories

"Success is never final." ~ Winston Churchill

"If you are the cause of the problem, then you are the solution." ~ unknown

"Even if you're on the right track, you'll still get run over if you just sit there." ~ Will Rogers

"The power to shape the future is earned through persistence. No other quality is as essential to success. . . . It is the ability to move mountains one grain of sand at a time." ~ Successories

"Although they think strategically to solve problems outside of school, it doesn't occur to some students to use the same type of thinking and questioning when they study." ~ Cynthia M. Schmidt

B. Tackling Schoolwork

Here again is an opportunity for your students to think about and assess how they conduct their academic lives. Do they plan ahead, survey text, and establish a mindset before reading, or are they focused only on getting it over with—even mindlessly? Does an adult have to supervise their work or are they self-starters? Are they last-minute folks or do they review material periodically? The emphasis here should be on an honest appraisal—not pat, teacher-approved responses.

After going through the items, students should add up their checkmarks and record their total. Sharing should follow, as each statement represents a weak area.

C. Getting Started

This activity prepares the way for Francis Robinson's SQ3R study method, starting with surveying. Consider this a reality check: how much do your students know about their textbooks, its layout and special provisions? (A textbook survey activity follows on the next page.) You can do this together, step-by-step, discussing as you go along or have students work on their own, sharing and discussing upon completion. You may very well find that many students don't know their text's copyright date or its implications, let alone the contents of its appendix. Poll results.

D. A Man Named Robinson/Keep on Surveying

1. Write SQ3R on the board and ask students to jot down everything they know about it. Hopefully, most will be familiar with this classic study method, but that is not always the case.

2. After reading the introductory paragraph to your students, you might want to share a few of your own schooling experiences—mistakes, disappointments, successes, etc. No one ever taught me how to study—and I certainly could have used the advice!

3. You might also want to preface this textbook survey by asking such questions as, "When you are first given a text during those first days of school and before any readings have been assigned, what, if anything, do you do with it?" Some may very well tell you that they simply cover it, never so much as taking a glance inside. Remind students how essential it is to know their text well and then begin the survey.

E. Chapter Surveying

It is also essential for children to look over a chapter before reading it, gathering some ideas/impressions about the topic, thus triggering prior knowledge. Unfortunately, in their haste to complete the reading and respond to end-of-chapter questions, many children ignore this step doing themselves a disservice. Go over this activity together and point out the Harvard study at the bottom of the page.

F. The All-Important "Q"

1. The art of question-making cannot be emphasized enough. Model this skill repeatedly and help children distinguish between main ideas, important details, and "fluff." As you do so, focus on the format of most text chapters: headings, sub-headings, summaries, end-of-chapter questions, and review activities. Remind students to look these over first.

2. Demonstrate two-column note-taking, showing students how to fold their notebook paper to create a left-hand margin of about 2½ inches. This is where, in abbreviated form, their questions are to be recorded. Although Robinson advises that questions be noted before the chapter is read, some students prefer to record both their questions and answers while reading. Whatever suits their working style is best. The goal here is to create a useful study guide.

3. Review the five W's and H—who, what, where, when, why, and how—for turning headings and main ideas (usually found in the first sentence of textbook paragraphs) into questions. All notes should be abbreviated and more practice is provided here. Share results.

4. Many children may resist the notion of taking textbook notes, thinking it faster to just read—even reread—a chapter and then hunt for answers. This, of course, is not the case, but you may have to do

some convincing. Let's face it, the prospect of taking such notes can seem monumental. Once this unit has been completed, creat two-column study guides with your students or even for them, at least for a while. Students will then read actively, searching for and recording answers. When studying, the paper is simply folded over so only the questions are revealed. These are then answered out loud—but when stumped, the correct answer is just on the other side, to be recited before making another attempt. A test or two will prove the usefulness of these self-generated study guides. And just think what they'll mean at final exam time! As grades improve, your students will be hooked, and they'll soon take over the entire task, moving on as fully independent learners.

5. Suggest that lecture and film notes be written using the same two-column format, only in reverse, with questions being added afterward.

H. Sample Two-Column Notes

Now comes a bit of practice. This activity can be done individually, or the sample can be enlarged and placed on an overhead for whole class "translating." Respond to questions as you proceed and encourage students to refer back to the abbreviations in the note-taking unit if necessary. Note that the original text is provided. Discourage discouragement; after all, when they're the abbreviator, their notes will definitely make sense to them.

If you prefer, give the students the text and have them abbreviate it, comparing their renditions with the sample provided.

I. Last Steps

This page explains in some detail the three R's of Robinson's study method. Be sure to emphasize the importance of recitation—studying out loud, "teaching a pillow," so to speak, hence using all their senses to learn and own the material. Recitation is considered the most effective study technique around, while the act of writing questions and answers initiates this learning process. Explain that this is the reason teachers seldom have to refer to their notes when conducting class—especially after first period. We've now written it, seen it, spoken and heard it repeatedly. It's now ours.

And repetition, a key memory technique detailed in the next unit, is the essence of reviewing. Cramming does not lead to ownership. Instead, it results in forgetting, much frustration, and even despair on the part of many children.

J. Reasons for Moving West/Two-Column Practice

1. This activity, based on a selection from *Many Americans—One Nation* allows children to again try their hand at two-column note-taking. Encourage students to quickly survey the passage and note the headings and main ideas.

2. On the next page, students should jot down their questions. Actually, there is only one question answered in this passage: Why did the settlers move west? This, of course can be abbreviated to: Why → west? or even: → west?

3. Then comes the answering piece, with abbreviated answers recorded to the right of the question.

4. Notes can then be compared, ways of improving notes and abbreviating even more, and concerns addressed. Yes/No questions are provided as is a rating scale.

5. Once completed, give students a few minutes to quietly whisper-read their notes, with the intention of learning them. Repeat this for another day or two and then, as a follow-up a few days hence, ask

them to write down the reasons settlers chose to move westward. I'm banking on their knowing all of them!

6. Provide students with plenty of duplicated textbook pages to practice and evaluate their highlighting, as well as their two-column notes.

7. As mentioned previously, to keep the momentum going, consider helping students by providing them with prepared two-column text notes questions based on their coursework.

Part 7: Memory Technique Activities

A. Board Quotes

"A man's real possession is his memory. In nothing else is he rich, in nothing else is he poor." ~ Alexander Smith

"Memory is the diary we all carry about with us." ~ Oscar Wilde

"To the memory, nothing is ever really lost." ~ Eudora Welty

"When people say, 'I forgot,' usually they didn't. What really happened is that they didn't know it in the first place." ~ Jerry Lucas

"All memory, whether trained or untrained, is based on association." ~ Jerry Lucas

"It's always easier to remember things that have meaning than to remember things that do not." ~ Jerry Lucas

"If we see or hear something exceptionally base, dishonorable, great, unbelievable, or ridiculous, we are likely to remember it for a long time. It stirs the mind." ~ Jerry Lucas

"According to researchers, brain images taken during IQ testing show that most mental activity appears centered on a handful of golf-ball-size spots near the front of the brain." ~ Dan Vergano, *USA Today*

"Like an umbrella, the mind works better when it's open." ~ Jerry Lynch

B. Your SQ3R Checklist

Consider this a reference and reminder page to be used as a checklist as students continue to follow Robinson's lead.

C. A True Story

We all seem to underestimate our propensity for forgetting, while overestimating our capacity to remember with just a quick read or hearing. This is unfortunate but true tale launches this memory unit, drawing a comparison between our minds and computers, and the risks involved when we fail to take steps to "save" information—be it on our hard drives or long-term memories. Every one of us has experienced the horror of forgetting on a test what we "knew" so well the night before. The accompanying phone number activity demonstrates the fallibility of our short-term, or working, memories. Since phone books won't be handy, simply write a phone number on the board and quickly erase it, shutting the phone book as it were. Then, before allowing students to record the number, delay for a minute or two, as if dialing the number and getting a busy signal. Some will recall it, but most will not. This, of course, underscores the importance of writing things down and rehearsing them in order to secure them in our minds.

D. Dial Away!

   1. This is a fun way to reinforce the point made on the previous page. Many children, adults too, mislead themselves into believing that repetition alone is sufficient for remembering. "Who needs to write it down? I'll remember it," they proclaim. Well, let's just see about that with this phone dial activity. Contrary to their claims, most students will err when they attempt to recreate all the numbers and letters on the buttons, underscoring the memory rule of *focused* repetition and the fact that writing things down initiates and promotes learning.

E. Uh, Oh!

   1. Dr. Pedlow at the University of Maine taught me well the risks of last minute studying with these facts, reminding me (and now your students) about the forgetting curve mentioned previously in the note-taking unit. Unless we take appropriate measures, there's a good chance that what we thought we knew will fade to the tune of 95 percent in just four weeks! *Interference*—all those distractions that bombard us from the moment we turn out the lights and start dreaming to all the voices, sounds, and events that greet us during our waking hours—will further come between us and our memories. Your students need to know that.

   2. Ask students to talk about their afternoon classes. Anyone have his/her hardest course at the end of the day? Add a test to the brew of a day's worth of distractions, including a noisy lunch and fading energy, and you've got a problem. Kids will understand immediately.

   3. And just to prove the point that our minds have minds of their own, letting us down at every turn, there is this Question and Answer activity. Most of your students will fill in the blank with "yolk." Few, if any, will think *albumin*. Point taken.

F. Brainy Facts

As big as the state of Texas and 100 stories tall. . . . The brain is a most intriguing organ, and students should know that and be curious to learn more about this cranial control center. These ten brainy facts should impress your students, as they check off those they are already familiar with. Most will be amazed at our brain's incredible capacity—and how little of it we use. Children need to be reminded that this three pound dynamo expends about one-fourth of all our energy, is more powerful than any computer, generates a good deal of electricity, and needs to be well-rested and nourished. As my dad liked to say, "You are what you eat!" Anyone for spinach?

G. Information Overload

   1. Ask students to flip through their notebook(s) and take a look at class notes and, if applicable, vocabulary lists. Then ask how they go about studying all of this information. Hopefully, now many notes will be in two-column format. If not, these next activities will underscore their usefulness. As for pages filled with lists of vocabulary words, definitions, even parts of speech and accompanying sentences, it's just too much for the brain to handle. Enter *chunking* . . .

   2. Chunking means grouping information that is to be learned in some meaningful way. You might want to have already written the first set of numbers on the board, kept hidden, perhaps, behind a screen. Reveal them for about 30 seconds and then cover them up again. Add a minute of distracting talk and then ask students to write down the number in exact order. Most will be unsuccessful—and that's just fine.

Then group the numbers by dates and repeat the same steps. This time, success will reign, proving the point. More sets of numbers are provided for practice, and you can create more.

3. Provide students with flash cards and, if necessary, demonstrate how to use them. For instance, show students a pack of five or six prepared vocabulary or date/event flash cards and proceed to flip through them, reciting as you go. Pretend to be uncertain of a few, setting them aside for further review. Once assured that all are known, tackle the whole stack again, out loud. Flash cards, like Ma Bell, chunk information very effectively.

H. Remember This!/Chunk It!

These two activities go hand in hand. The first asks students to quickly memorize twenty words. To avoid peeking, provide a separate sheet of paper and also be sure to add a distracting comment or two. Most will do dismally. "Chunk It," however, categorizes those same words, hence making memorization and retention much easier. This reinforces our third memory rule that grouping information in a meaningful way promotes learning and recall. When children attempt it and meet success, you've made your sale. Share thoughts and results.

I. Memory Games/Memory Remedies

1. These two activities demonstrate three more memory techniques: sentence cues, acronyms, and spelling mnemonics. Although some may already know the planets and the colors of the visible spectrum as well as the spelling of these four words, many won't. The important thing is that they serve as a vehicle for explaining how to apply these tools to learning. Give students two minutes to memorize these items and then cover them up. Again, add a bit of distracting talk and then test them. Share comments and results.

2. "Memory Remedies" presents a planetary sentence cue, spectrum acronym, and four spelling mnemonics. For all your musicians, ask how they learned the notes on the lines and spaces of the treble clef: All Good Boys Do Fine; F-A-C-E.

    Again, after two minutes, distract, retest, and share scores. Most will improve markedly.

J. Your Turn Again/Drawing Comparisons

This first activity requires that your students apply what they've learned, creating their own memory aids. Have them then share their work before comparing it with mine on the following page's "Drawing Comparisons." Discussion should follow, with the reminder that there is no "right" answer—only what serves their memories best.

K. Quizzing

1. Here's an opportunity for students to study the memory aids they devised or borrowed and then be tested. Self-scoring can follow, results shared, as they discuss what they did and experienced.

2. Flip through textbooks and offer more practice with memory aids, such as:

    a) the five Prairie Indian tribes (Sioux, Cheyenne, Pawnee, Chippewa and Fox) and the four Plains Indian tribes (Hidatsa, Arapaho, Comanche, and Mandan)

    b) the five layers of the scalp (pericranium, loose connective tissue, aponeurosis, close connective tissue, and skin)

    c) the first ten presidents (Washington, J. Adams, Jefferson, Madison, Monroe, J. Q. Adams, Jackson, Van Buren, Harrison, and Tyler)

    d) the parts of a microscope (eyepiece, body tube, arm, nosepiece, high power objective, low power objective, coarse adjustment, stage clips, stage, diaphragm, mirror or light, and base)

3. Have students share words they find hard to spell and, either in groups or with the whole class, create spelling mnemonics.

L. A Picture Is Worth a Thousand Words!

1. Another powerful memory technique is imaging, using the "mind's eye" to visualize and hence remember information. Start by asking if anyone has ever read a book and then seen the film version only to be disappointed in the portrayal of the characters. They just didn't look right because that's not how they were "pictured" during the reading. When reading, plots and characters quite literally play in our minds like a movie, and we often feel as if we actually know them. That's the power of mind's eye. For some it comes quite easily; others need practice, especially reluctant readers who under-use their imaginations.

2. You can either read this abbreviated version of "The Fox and the Crow," or have it read silently. Afterward, students should jot down what they "saw" during the story, illustrate it, and share. This lays the foundation for applying mind's eye imaging to content-area material.

3. Here is an additional imaging activity you might want to try:

    a) Darken the room, using only a flashlight or candle to see by, and ask students to close their eyes. After taking a deep breath or two and relaxing, ask them to visualize an apple, turning it around in their mind's eye, looking at it every which way. Then ask them to draw and/or describe their apple in detail and share what they "saw."

    b) Clear their minds and this time, ask them to visualize an old person. Where is this person? What is s/he doing? Looking like? Etc. Then again have them draw and/or describe what they "saw." (You can also have them "see" themselves as very young children, or studying, coupled with some positive self-talk, and so on). Most students will enjoy this quiet, creative activity.

M. A Mind's Eye Science Lesson

1. This page presents a selection from *Science Connections* (Merrill Publishing Co., 1990). Remind students to create a mental image of the information. Once finished, they should jot down whatever they "saw." Then ask for explanations. Flash cards can be made, followed by a brief, whisper-recited, review and quiz. Sharing and discussion should follow. It's important to provide students with opportunities to reflect about their own thinking process.

2. Provide other such opportunities, encouraging students to use as many of the memory aids shared in this unit as will accomplish their task: writing as in two-column notes, flash cards, reciting, imaging, and so on. Over time, talk about their experiences, as they go on to enhance the way they study.

N. A Memory Test/The Memory Test Continues

This "test" is a fun way to reinforce some of the memory techniques mentioned in this unit. After reminding students of that, give them just two minutes to memorize all the pictured items. When time is up, have them turn to the next page and start in with a bit of distracting conversation. Then give them a chance to record whatever they can recall. Once done, let them check their list with the pictures, record their total, and share the techniques they used. Give them another chance or two to rehearse and, if need be, change tactics, thus adding repetition to the mix and see what happens by quizzing them in a day or two—even longer. I think they will be impressed with themselves.

O. More Memory Facts and Tips

1. Control. Sometimes we feel like victims of our circumstances. I surely know a number of children who feel powerless in the face of academic demands to internalize and memorize huge amounts of information for later testing—not to mention finals. That's why it's important to help children recognize the proven steps that will give them an academic edge. Some of these tips they are already familiar with, such as making a note of things, and hopefully they are now all doing just that. Others may be quite novel. Read each item to your class as they check off unknown items and then discuss.

2. As a journal entry or on a separate sheet of paper, ask students, without looking up, to jot down every detail of your classroom they can recall and share. The details recalled during this brain exercise will be quite illuminating.

3. Follow that with these questions for discussion:
    a) Typical breakfast?
    b) Typical lunch?
    c) Favorite snack foods?
    d) Types of exercise engage in?
    e) Ever panic on a test? When? How often? Its impact on success?
    f) Ever remember the words to a long-ago song?
    g) Ever engage in word games, puzzles? (This last question sets the stage for this unit's concluding pages. . . .)

P. Word Play

Just like the childhood party game, this activity asks students to make as many words as they can, relying solely on the letters in *transportation*. There are actually more than 200 of them! Such word play exercises the brain and improves concentration. Try it with other words, too, and keep a supply of word searches, crossword puzzles, etc. on hand.

Q. Brain Teasers/Keep Exercising!

1. These two pages represent a mental workout for your students. There should be no collaborating or peeking at the answers provided on that second page. In fact, don't even mention them. They'll discover them soon enough. Explain any that remain confusing.

2. My students supplied many of these to me, and you will probably be able to gather a wealth of brain teasers from yours, too.

Part 8: Testwiseness Activities

A. Board Quotes

"Improve your performance by improving your attitude." ~ Argus

"There will be failure; there is failure and there is judgment. You can be told you did a lousy job. You can be fired." ~ Marshall Duke, Ph.D.

"Failure provides the needed contrast that makes success all the sweeter when it happens." ~ Marshall Duke, Ph.D.

"Sleep is just as important as food and water. It's time it's treated that way." ~ Joyce A. Waslleben, Ph.D.

"If you're sleepy during the day, then you're probably not getting enough." ~ Gary S. Richardson, M.D.

"Do you think *sorry* landed a man on the moon?" ~ unknown

"True intelligence is not just how well you perform on a test; it's how well you perform in life." ~ unknown

"Strive for excellence, not perfection." ~ unknown

"Don't make excuses; make improvements." ~ Argus

"Let your efforts rise above your excuses." ~ Argus

"If you have made mistakes . . . there is always another chance for you. You may have a fresh start any time you choose." ~ Mary Pickford

"You can't possibly hit the ball if you're thinking about all the possible ways you can miss." ~ unknown

"An error doesn't become a mistake until you refuse to correct it." ~ John Entemann

"It is better to ask the way fifty times than to take the wrong road once." ~ Jewish saying

"You can't learn unless you ask questions." ~ Oliver Wendell Holmes

"Even Einstein asked questions." ~ Argus

"Those who don't stop asking silly questions become scientists." ~ unknown

"He who asks a question is a fool for five minutes; he who fails to ask his question is a fool forever." ~ Chinese proverb

"Ask questions. It is one of the most important ways to improve your mind." ~ unknown

"All the fun is in how you say a thing." ~ Robert Frost

"Use strong verbs. One good verb is better at description than a clutter of adjectives and adverbs." ~ Joan Lowery Nixon

"Reading and writing are both composing processes in which the reader or writer constructs and re-constructs meaning." ~ Cynthia Chamblee

"Use as many words as you need and not one that you can get by without." ~ Robert Jordon

"The writer is careful of what he reads, for that is what he will write. He is careful of what he learns, for that is what he will know." ~ Annie Dillard

B. Take a Test Drive

1. Bob Chase, President of the NEA, writes that, according to psychologists, many people experience the same two recurring nightmares: we're either walking down a street naked or we're in school and having to take a test we're totally unprepared for. Let's face it, even when we've studied, uncertainty plagues many of us, heightening anxiety and undermining both confidence and recall. In this thoughtshot activity, students are given an opportunity to reveal their own test-taking issues. Expect such words as *pressure, failure, hatred, disappointment,* even *boring.* It will be a rare child who looks forward to and enjoys tests. Discussion should follow, as together you examine test-taking and the problems they often present. Share personal stories here, as well. Ever blank out? Claim to be sick in order to stay home? Etc.

2. Be sure to reiterate the role of anxiety in performance and its triggers, including lack of preparation, insecurity, track record, concept confusion, and so on. Remind students that a *little* anxiety is actually good, as it keeps us sharp. Too much, of course, leads to panic and often a dismal showing. Too little, on the other hand, suggests lack of caring. Best antidote: asking questions and preparation!

3. Afterward, instruct students to rate themselves as test-takers in each of their major subjects, and to explain the results. Few will rate themselves equally across the board, and reasons will probably include comfort level with the teacher, interest, teacher reviews, and test formats. Some teachers' tests may simply be viewed as being easier/fairer than others. Sharing should follow.

4. Now is also a good time to demonstrate that the true purpose of tests is to serve as a measure of knowledge and understanding. To that end, hand out paper on which to draw a line that is, say, $4\,\tfrac{3}{8}$" long. No rulers are allowed at this point but be assured that everyone will want one.

Then repeat the same instructions, except this time provide only half the class with a ruler. Expect some protest from the rest. How else can they assess accuracy? That, of course, is the whole point of this exercise. Tests are like rulers, except that, instead of measuring length, they measure what we know and still don't know. Tests are also an indirect teaching tool, a measure of how successful we've been in our efforts to inform.

C. Food for Thought

1. In many instances, children have definite goals and care deeply about school and their futures. Some, however, are more shortsighted. Here, students reflect on who is more committed to their success—they or their parents—and why. As they share their insights and reaffirm life goals, remind them of the perennial hope that each generation will enjoy more advantages than the one before it. That, of course, is more likely with a good education, what my father called a "life gift."

2. The January 6, 2000, *USA Today* Snapshot, "Education and pay," (see appendix) is based on Census Bureau findings and shows that an adult without a high school diploma earns only about $16,124. Add the diploma and that figure jumps to $22,895. As for college, a graduate with an associate's degree can expect to earn about $29,872; with a bachelor's degree, income tops the $40,000 mark. These facts of life are sure to catch someone's attention.

However, education does far more than provide a financial edge; it offers choices. Ask your students if they know anyone who dislikes their job, dreading mornings and trudging off to work, feeling undervalued and/or underpaid. Perhaps that same person regrets not being better educated, seeing no way out of his/her situation because they simply don't qualify for much else—especially in this technology-driven age where there is a premium on communication skills. As you talk together, emphasize the importance of choices and loving one's work, regardless of status and salary.

3. Such conversations can be quite illuminating, particularly for children who see little value in education. Money, after all, is a powerful motivator. So is dream fulfillment. And that is where all of this is heading, right to *motivation.* Explain to students that the root word *mot-* is Latin for "move," and that's what you want to know: what motivates them—gets them moving. To that end, have everyone check off their motivators, adding any that don't appear on the list.

4. During your follow-up discussion, delve into the three words defined on this page: *competition, self-confidence,* and *self-esteem.* The first, of course, is a motivator too, as we challenge ourselves to outdo our neighbors, colleagues, friends—some even resorting to cheating in order to win the prize. The next page is devoted to that topic.

Remind students, too, of the distinction between self-confidence and self-esteem. The former suggests a belief in one's ability, while the former represents a self-liking. Of course, in many ways, they can go hand-in-hand. The point is that confidence improves with success, something that often requires hard work. And the meeting of such challenges is what earns our self-respect, our self-esteem—even if we fail.

D. At a High Cost

1. This activity requires total honesty as students answer these seven questions. Hopefully, the comfort level is high among your students so that sharing can follow. First, however, simply talk about cheating, and all its various forms, everything from taxes to tests. Copying, too. Share *USA Today*'s "Epidemic of cheating" in the appendix. Also mention that in the January 15 , 2001 *USA Today* Snapshot, "Cheating Students," it was found that, among teens who rank at the top of their classes, 78 percent said they had cheated in school; 39 percent said they'd cheated on a test; 65 percent reported copying someone else's homework.

2. Then offer up the example of Senator Joe Biden. When seeking the presidency years ago, word leaked that during his first year at Syracuse University Law School, he was accused of plagiarism and called before the school's disciplinary body. An academic official then reported that Biden had been found guilty; he then begged for another chance, promising never to repeat his mistake. Needless to say, he never kept that promise nor did he win his party's nomination. He also used, without permission, the words of British politician, Neil Kinnock. That was followed by more revelations of plagiarism, including a speech made by Robert Kennedy when running for president in 1968:

   "The gross national product does not allow for the health of our children, the quality of their education or the joy of their play. It does not include the beauty of our poetry, or the strength of our marriages, the intelligence of our public debate or the integrity of our public officials.

   It measures neither our wit nor our courage, neither our wisdom nor our devotion to our country. It measures everything, in short, except that which makes life worthwhile, and it can tell us everything about America except why we are proud that we are Americans."

   Here's Joe Biden's speech to the California State Democratic Convention denouncing American's materialism:

   "We cannot measure the health of our children, the quality of their education, the joy of their play," adding that an economic statistic "doesn't measure the beauty of our poetry, the strength of our marriages, the intelligence of our public debate, the integrity of our public officials.

   It counts neither our wit nor our wisdom, neither our compassion nor our devotion to our country. . . . The bottom line can tell us everything about our lives except that which makes life worthwhile, and it can tell us everything about America except that which makes us proud to be Americans."

   ***Rumor has it that Biden still aspires to the presidency.

3. In March 2000, Pennsylvania author, Nancy Stouffer, sued J. K Rowlings and her publishers, claiming that plots and characters in the wildly popular Harry Potter series were lifted from her *Legend of Rah and Muggles*, which included among other similarities, a character named Larry Potter. As Stouffer said, "I think coincidences happen, but if it looks like a duck and acts like a duck, it's a duck."

4. On January 22, 2001, the United States Supreme Court rejected singer Michael Bolton and his record company's appeal to overturn a $5.4 million jury verdict that his hit song, *Love Is a Wonderful Thing*, was partly copied from an Isley Brothers song with the same name.

5. Talk about *honor* and *trust*, which, once broken, is rarely repaired. Share your own stories as a student and teacher. Explain how prevalent cheating and copying are and how wrong—even if we get away with it. Come back to that idea of self-respect and confidence. If we had those, this conversation would be unnecessary. Ditto for some test-taking strategies, which is what this unit is devoted to.

E. Me and Test Taking

1. It's important to first assess how students currently approach, tackle, and perform on tests. Talk about each item as students check off those that apply to them. Once completed, find out, by a show of hands, how many checked off at least three items, thus underscoring the need for help and change.

2. Again, remind students that too much anxiety wreaks havoc on performance, while too little suggest lack of preparation and caring. All it takes is a little to keep us on our toes, thus improving our odds.

F. Being Objective

Focusing first on objective tests only, this activity will help you assess how much your students already know about them. Please note that the first five are false; all the rest are true. As you discuss each item, be sure that, when you reach #4 and #5 you explain the difference between wild and educated guessing, and the importance of reading and listening to all directions before jumping right in. For instance, a colleague of mine insists that the words *true* and *false* be written out. Miss that piece of information, abbreviate, and fail! Once done, poll to see how your students scored.

G. Test Prep

Each of these items is a review tip, with several harkening back to prior units. Remind students to respond honestly, and then, as discussion winds down, survey the class and have students record those they need to incorporate when preparing for a test. In their journals or notebook Action Plan sheet (see appendix), these should be written out and revisited from time to time.

H. Being Testwise

1. Some of these have already been addressed fully, so target those that are new or bear repeating:
    a) Confidence comes from being well-prepared: listening and taking class and text notes, reciting and frequent reviewing.
    b) Arriving late for class leaves students winded and tense when they should be settling in for the test.
    c) This is not the time to discover a broken pencil point or no writing instrument at all!
    d) Last minute, test-related conversations should be avoided as the risk is too great that misinformation will be shared or that a memory lapse will trigger panic.
    e) Ignoring teacher instructions is costly, as they often clarify or modify directions and note additions/corrections.
    f) Establishing a test mind-set requires a brief perusal of the entire test (after attending to directions) to determine what to expect, what's expected, and how to plan time.
    g) Ignore direction words, such as "Which one is NOT correct," and lose points.
    h) Answering easier questions not only builds confidence but insures that whatever can be answered has been before time runs out. What if the easiest question is the last one and you never get that far? Moreover, some questions reveal answers to harder ones.
    i) Getting stuck on a particularly difficult question wastes time. Instead, these should be marked faintly and skipped until all questions have been tackled.
    j) Students don't always realize how much they actually know. After all, they've been listening to and reading about this topic for a while, and it's this knowledge that they need to draw on when guessing. Educated guessing, that is, not wild, thoughtless guessing.
    k) Students, afraid of being wrong, sometimes leave an item unanswered. At that point, even a wild guess makes more sense.

l) Ask if anyone has ever changed a correct answer to a wrong one. It happens all the time. Best advice: don't change anything unless positive it's an error. Research suggests that our first response is usually right.

m) Remind students that, if you can't read their writing, you can't grade it!

n) Find out if any students have ever rushed through a test because it seems as if everyone else is finishing up, and they don't want to be last. Remind students to take advantage of the allotted time and use as much of it as they need. Being first done doesn't necessarily mean I know it all; indeed, it may very well mean just the opposite. Other test-takers should be ignored; they can be very unsettling.

2. Again, emphasize goals as students add up their checkmarks and decide which items they need to be mindful of in testing situations. These should then be recorded in their journals or action plan sheets (see appendix).

I. The Rest of the Story

1. Too many children jam returned tests into notebooks, texts, or even the waste can. Keeping in mind that tests are measuring/learning tools, encourage students to assess their test performances with the items posed here. Once returned, tests should always be corrected and reflected upon. After all, they represent much of the important information on a particular topic.

2. Students also need to be reminded that when they are unsure of what they did wrong on a test or are still confused about the topic, they need to go straight to that teacher. No excuses.

J. It Takes Two

This Venn diagram activity asks students to compare/contrast objective and essay tests, recording similarities in the center area shared by both ovals. Then find out their preference and why. It should be noted that many teachers prefer objective tests, despite the time it takes to prepare them. Grading is so much faster—and objective! Many experts believe, however, that essays are superior, requiring a solid knowledge base for deep coverage of a topic, coupled with organization and writing skills. Both types of tests are treated in detail on the following pages.

K. Multiple Choice Test Tips/More Multiple Choice Tips/Even More M.C. Tips

Students should highlight unfamiliar tips, as you go over each one. Key points to emphasize:

- Children are often misled when their anticipated answer comes first, thus ignoring all other options, ignoring that more than one might be correct.
- Show students how to eliminate options, providing them with countless examples in addition to those provided here in #6, 7, 8, 9, 11, 12, and 14.
- Explain how teachers often insert a "decoy" option—one that is *almost* but not completely correct. Students jump at these, as teachers well know. This is one reason objective tests are not always a good indicator of what a child knows.
- Research suggests that the option, "All of the above are correct," is usually the right answer. Also, even if only fairly certain that none of the options is correct, the best response is "None of the above."
- It bears repeating that difficult items should be marked faintly and skipped until the end, if time allows. And make those educated, not wild, guesses.
- Since tests are measures, instruct students to star those they guessed at, so when tests are returned, they can gauge the accuracy of their hunches.

L. A New Approach

Multiple choice tests are taken more than any other kind and so requires an action plan. Have students run through all the tips on the three previous pages and those they need to be mindful of whenever encountering such tests. Discussion should then follow.

M. On Being True or False/More on T/F Tests

1. Many children claim true/false tests as their favorite type, saying they like having that 50-50 chance of being right—but they should beware. Naturally, many of the already-mentioned tips apply here, everything from pacing, skipping bothersome questions, and making educated guesses. Review these and emphasize #7 which highlights the role of *specific determiners* and their implication that a statement is very likely false, whereas such words as *sometimes, probably,* and *usually* suggest a true statement.

2. Also stress the significance of the relationship between the ideas expressed in a question and critical words, such as *since* and *because of.* These suggest a causal relationship between two true statements that may not actually exist, as indicated in #9. Provide plenty of examples to insure understanding, emphasizing that, to be true, the statement must be true in its entirety. Moreover, as #11 details, longer statements may very well be false, as all it takes is one word to make an otherwise true statement false.

3. Finally, remind children *not* to look for or be influenced by response patterns. We all like balance, so we are put off when a majority of our answers lean one way or the other, thus causing us to change a one or two. There are no patterns, and students must simply accept that as fact!

4. Once completed, instruct students to note the five tips they deem most crucial to their success on true/false tests and share their reasoning.

N. The Matching Game

1. As always, easiest items should be tackled first. Moreover, on these tests, capital letters are best—less chance of misrepresentation. Some tips, such as crossing off used options, are second nature to most students; others might not be so familiar. These include using parts of speech and capitalized words to good advantage. The same can be said for reading the phrases/definitions before the term on vocabulary tests, and matching names with events and/or events with dates on history tests.

2. Also remind students that teachers will sometimes go out of their way not to place a stem right beside its correct option, and that we often, at the last minute, decide to tack on filler options at the end of the second column. As a result, they should focus on options in the middle of the list when unsure of an answer.

O. One More Match-Up

1. There are three things that teachers can do to "ruin" a perfectly good matching test. Are your students aware of what you're capable of? Answers are provided at the bottom of the page: 1) options can be used more than once; 2) "None of the above" can be included as an option; and 3) columns can be uneven in number. Discuss these possibilities and quickly learn what your students have been presented with.

2. Then give your students an opportunity to devise a matching test for a fellow student based on a current topic under study. These can then be "graded" and discussed. Did anyone exercise their right to make things difficult for a classmate? Were their tests fair? Etc.

P. Testing, 1, 2, 3/Testing, 4, 5, 6

Answers are provided at the end for self-correcting this objective test-taking quiz, and your students' chances of acing it will vastly improve if they are mindful of all the tips presented so far. This, then, serves as a review and assessment of their current testwiseness. Poll their success rate before moving on.

Q. One Versus the Other

1. Before addressing this page, ask students to think back to the Venn diagram they completed on page 130 and then jot down on a separate sheet of paper all the distinctions they can between objective and essay tests. Then focus on essay tests in detail, as noted here, emphasizing their advantages, while acknowledging the difficulties some students have in organizing their thoughts and writing a comprehensive, cohesive response.

2. In preparation for the next activity, ask students to define such words as *compare, contrast,* and *prove.* Some will be right on target, but many won't be, thus leading into the direction word inventory that follows.

R. Direction Word Inventory/Those Direction Words Defined

Have students take this matching "test," noting that the columns are evenly matched in number. Then have them do a self-check on the next page and score themselves. Poll the success rate, hand out flash cards, and instruct students to complete one for every missed term. Schedule a quiz a few days hence, allowing for some recited review sessions beforehand

S. The Art of Essaying

1. Carefully go over each item as students highlight unfamiliar tips. Time constraints are particularly crucial here. Spend too much time on one question and you will fail to respond to another—even though you know the answer! Unlike objective tests, hasty educated guesses will be of little service. Point out, too, that teachers often offer choices, such as asking students to answer two of the four posed questions. Miss that vital piece of information, valiantly trying to respond to all of them, and pay a dear price.

2. Jotting down an ordered outline beforehand will keep students focused on the topic, insuring that all vital information is included and in logical sequence, while avoiding the risk of straying into unrelated or non-essential details.

3. Although we regularly instruct students to turn the question into the introductory sentence, the importance of coming up with a strong lead sentence and paragraph also needs to be addressed. Number eleven provides an example, as does the next activity, "Practice Leading." Here are a few more, all from the pages of *USA Today*:

On the May 1999 Oklahoma tornado: "The killer was born high above the Earth it would devastate, the spawn of hot, rising air from the South and the cold, sinking air from the West. It was just a storm, but to those who ran from its dark tentacles or cowered under its howling fury, it was a monster, loud as Hell, black as Death."

On the ongoing Sudanese civil war: "In the year that they ate leaves, Emmanuel was four. The civil war in Sudan had come to his home in Kongor, scattering its people. He fled, carrying his baby sister in his arms, and never saw his parents again."

On the inauguration of George W. Bush (1/19–21/01): "For George W. Bush, moving into the White House on Saturday is like regaining the family business eight years after a hostile take-over put it in outsiders' hands."

T. Practice Leading

   1. In this activity, lead sentences accompany four topics—all written by middle-schoolers. Ask your students to evaluate them. Which is the most/least effective and why?

   2. Now it's your students' turn to try their hand at leading. Their topic: cockroaches! Several roach-related facts are provided. Their task is to read them carefully and then come up with a fairly general lead sentence designed to introduce the subject, while catching the reader's attention and inviting him/her to read on. After revising and editing, have students share and critique their work looking for ways to improve on it.

U. Did You Know That . . .

Here are some interesting historical events dating from 1895 with the invention of the safety razor and its disposable blades to the 1945 bombing of Hiroshima and Nagasaki. Ask students to record their three favorites.

V. Go Searching

Once students have narrowed their three favorite topics down to one, they need to now do some library and/or Internet research. Several accompanying questions serve to guide their searches, as is space for the recording of uncovered facts and details. Once completed, they'll be ready to put it all together on the next page.

W. In the Lead/What Your Teachers Look For (And So Should You!)

   1. To start things off, a sample lead paragraph is provided, this one written by a a seventh grader. Again, after sharing it with your class, ask students to critique it. What do they like about it? What, if anything, would they change? Etc. Then it's their turn.

   2. After noting their most important/interesting facts and details from the previous page, they are to write their lead sentence and introductory paragraph. This, of course, will represent only their first draft. Unlike essay tests, here they have an opportunity to share their efforts with a classmate, revising to make it more effective, and correcting any mechanical errors. A checklist is offered on the next page.

   3. The polished final version should be written on a separate sheet of paper and shared with the whole class, both for its writing merits and the new learning it reflects.

X. Mistakes To Learn From

As students take tests for you and other teachers, they need to carry with them all the study techniques and testwise tips you've shared with them. For now, ask students to reflect on a recent test and then check off the "mistakes" they made when preparing and/or taking it. These can then be shared and discussed.

Y. Once Over Lightly

   1. This final activity serves to pull all of your students' newly gained testwise strategies and remaining pitfalls together, as they follow up with promised improvements. These can then be shared and referred to often.

   2. As a review technique or clarifying strategy, engage your students in C. Burke's "Written Conversations." At the end of a unit of study, group students in pairs or triads and give each group paper and pencils. Explain that talking is NOT allowed and that all "conversations" must be entirely in writing, as they respond to your review questions, sharing, adding, and correcting as they proceed. Final results can then be presented as part of a whole class discussion and review.

Part 1

INTRODUCTORY ACTIVITIES

The Changeling Eagle

Like so many folktales, this Native American story about a changeling eagle teaches us a lesson about who and what we choose to be. Read it carefully and then, on the lines provided on the next page, jot down what you think that lesson is.

Once upon a time, a young Indian brave walking alone in the forest found an eagle's egg. Oddly enough, though, he mistook it for a prairie chicken egg and placed it in a prairie chicken's nest when he returned home. And so, the changeling eagle grew up thinking that he was a prairie chicken. Indeed, before long he was clucking like a chicken, walking like a chicken—living like a chicken. For that reason, flying was out of the question for him; all he could do was flail his wings, taking him upwards only a few feet at a time.

One bright morning, the changeling eagle looked up and saw the most wonderful sight: a large, graceful bird soaring through the sky, gliding among the clouds. The changeling eagle was dazzled by the sight and called to his mother, "Look! Look, Mother! Up in the sky! What is that beautiful bird?"

"Oh," she replied, as she looked up, "that's an eagle. Isn't she beautiful? Why, eagles are the fastest, most magnificent of all birds."

I wish I were an eagle, thought the young changeling. What fun to fly so gracefully, to be so handsome . . .

But as the days passed, the youngster soon forgot what he had seen. After all, his feet would always remain quite firmly on the ground, so why even dream about eagles and soaring through the air? And so he went on living as before, day in and day out, one season and year after another. Sadly, in all that time, the changeling never realized he was actually an eagle, and he died a prairie chicken.

"The Changeling Eagle" is trying to teach us that _____

_____

_____

_____

_____

 Share your thoughts with your classmates, teacher, and/or parent(s). See what meaning they take from this little tale. Are you all in agreement? What other ideas have been expressed?

_____

_____

_____

_____

Now that you understand what it means to be a changeling eagle and have decided not to follow his path, you're ready to make other choices, stretching to reach your potential. Let's begin.

ME AND MY FOLKS

*"Of all the relationships we experience, our relationship with
our parents is the first significant one." ~ Jane Brooks*

**DIRECTIONS: Think about it: You only spend about 13% of your time at
school. Most of it is spent at home with parents, so read the statements
below and check off those you already do.**

☐ When my parents say *"NO!"*, I realize they mean it and avoid a
power struggle.

☐ I occasionally tell my parent(s) that I love them.

☐ I, like my parent(s), have high expectations for myself.

☐ I offer to do chores that need doing before being asked.

☐ I sometimes ask to visit museums, libraries, theaters, zoos, etc.
with my parent(s).

☐ I often watch the news with my parent(s), as well as offerings
provided by the History and Discovery channels, etc.

☐ I'm interested in my parents' opinions about the news, entertainment, and/or music.

☐ I don't wait to be asked; instead I willingly share my day's
achievements, disappointments, and frustrations with my folks.

☐ I usually ask my parent(s) how their day is going.

☐ I help establish and contribute to family traditions and rituals.

☐ I invite my parents' help in balancing homework work, play, family,
friends, & rest.

☐ At least occasionally, I pack myself a healthy lunch.

*"If you have the courage to begin, you have
the courage to succeed." ~ David Viscott*

"Do your best at whatever you can. The world would be a
silent place if the only birds who sang were those who sang
the best." ~ unknown

ME AND MY FOLKS, Part II

DIRECTIONS: Looking back at the previous page, complete the T-Chart below, noting what you're already doing, together with improvements that need to be made.

Presently I . . .	Starting Right Now I . . .
1. _____	1. _____
_____	_____
2. _____	2. _____
_____	_____
3. _____	3. _____
_____	_____
4. _____	4. _____
_____	_____
5. _____	5. _____
_____	_____
6. _____	6. _____
_____	_____

Part 2

ORGANIZATION AND HOMEWORK ACTIVITIES

ACTUALLY . . .

How do you go about doing your work and completing tasks? Just answer TRUE/FALSE to find out.

_____ 1. I'm a last-minute kind of person.

_____ 2. My coat ends up wherever I happen to drop it.

_____ 3. I sometimes/often forget to record homework in my assignment book.

_____ 4. I don't record upcoming tests, projects, or reports on a large calendar displayed where I can readily see it.

_____ 5. I often rush through projects and reports, because I frequently forget about them until the night before.

_____ 6. I don't have a special place to store school supplies.

_____ 7. I seldom sort through my papers; I just let them pile up somewhere in my notebook, even my locker.

_____ 8. I throw away hand-outs, tests, etc. as soon as my teacher starts a new unit.

_____ 9. Sometimes I lose completed homework, so I can't hand it in when my teacher collects it.

_____10. I leave my stuff scattered about until the morning, and then I quickly gather it all up before leaving for school.

Scoring: If you answered TRUE to:
8–10 items: You need an immediate organization make-over.
4–7 items: An organization refresher course will set you on course.
1–3 items: A bit of reminding, and you'll be well on your way.

"Success is a journey, not a destination." ~ anonymous

TIPS ON GETTING ORGANIZED

DIRECTIONS: Here are some tips to help you organize your school materials. Place a check next to those you need to start doing and then jot them down on the spaces provided below.

- ☐ Never leave anything to the last minute—not homework, not studying for tests.
- ☐ Hang your coat or jacket on the same hook every day.
- ☐ Store sports and recreational equipment in a special container.
- ☐ Put up a big calendar identifying important dates, such as projects and reports.
- ☐ Establish a time-line, breaking a long-term assignment into manageable segments.
- ☐ Create a supply box, basket, shelf, or drawer filled with school supplies. (See page 41)
- ☐ Carry a separate, different-colored notebook for each major subject.
- ☐ Frequently sort through papers, filing them in the appropriate notebook sections.
- ☐ Keep a large notebook or box for storing completed units of study. Such papers will be needed for later assignments and preparing for final examinations.
- ☐ Put each completed assignment in a special homework folder, ready for turning in.
- ☐ Use the checklist on the next page to create a "Drop Spot," a place to gather all your school materials before going to bed, so that everything is in one place and ready to go with you the next morning.

ORGANIZING PLAN: I will . . .

1. _____

2. _____

3. _____

4. _____

5. _____

POST NEAR YOUR DROP SPOT:

- ☐ Books
- ☐ Notebook(s)
- ☐ Assignment Book
- ☐ Homework Folder
- ☐ Lunch money or lunch ready in fridge
- ☐ Permission slips, forms to be signed, etc.
- ☐ After-school items (sports gear, instruments, etc.)

"He that is good for making excuses is seldom good for anything else." ~
~ Benjamin Franklin

"If you fail to plan, you plan to fail." ~ Michelle Amodie

IN A BOX, BASKET, SHELF, OR DRAWER . . .

DIRECTIONS: *After checking off the items you already have on hand, make out a "shopping list."*

□ notebook paper
□ printer paper
□ construction paper
□ pencils/sharpener
□ colored pencils/crayons
□ erasers
□ pens
□ felt tip pens & markers
□ whiteout
□ ruler
□ scissors
□ highlighters
□ tape
□ glue or paste
□ hole punch
□ stapler/staples
□ paper clips
□ notebook dividers
□ index cards
□ thesaurus
□ dictionary
□ printer ink cartridges
□ hi-density computer discs

What I still need:

_____
_____
_____
_____
_____
_____
_____
_____
_____
_____
_____

> *"If you are the cause of the problem,*
> *then you are also the solution."* ~ unknown

School Life and You

"One of the biggest myths in education is that it's the teacher who accounts for learning, not you." ~ Ronald Gross

"It's a funny thing about life; if you refuse to accept anything but the best, you very often get it." ~ W. S. Maugham

DIRECTIONS: How do you conduct your school life? Check off those items that are already true for you, then highlight those you'll promise to try and jot them down below.

- ☐ I tell myself every day that I will work hard and learn from my mistakes, accepting nothing less than my best all the time.
- ☐ Instead of "I can't do this; it's too hard." I say, "I think I can; I'll sure try."
- ☐ I don't defend inappropriate behavior—not my own or anyone else's.
- ☐ I dress for success, looking neat and wearing well-fitting clothing, because I know appearance directly affects performance. Dress sloppily and you'll work sloppily.
- ☐ Even if I don't like a teacher, I try to learn as much as I can from her/him.
- ☐ I try to imitate successful students, watching what they do and following their lead.
- ☐ I ask questions in class, even if I think they're "dumb," because I know that questions lead to better understanding.
- ☐ I contribute to my classes, speaking up, asking, and answering questions.
- ☐ I don't blame others for my mistakes and never say things like, "I failed, because he's a lousy teacher!" "The teacher doesn't like me." "Everybody failed the test!"
- ☐ I accept my mistakes and learn from them, trying hard not to repeat them.
- ☐ I know it's one thing to fail but another not to figure out why and try to improve.
- ☐ I try not to be absent unless really sick. It's impossible to make up all that missed work!

PROMISES TO KEEP:

1. _____
2. _____
3. _____
4. _____
5. _____

"He who asks a question is a fool for five minutes. He who fails to ask is a fool forever."
~ Chinese Proverb

"Did you ever notice that athletes always raise the bar a little higher? They get better & better because they challenge themselves." ~ Walter Anderson

*** Eat breakfast and you'll work more efficiently, test better, and be more creative.

Homework: Getting It Right!

Here is the lowdown on homework. Do it all, and it's almost impossible to fail. Fail to do it, and, well, you know the rest of that story. To get you thinking about homework, look over these suggestions and check off those that target your work habits, so we can check on your homework credentials.

- ☐ I expect homework every day, including review sessions.
- ☐ I record all homework in an assignment book.
- ☐ I successfully balance my school work, leisure time, activities, family, friends, and rest.
- ☐ I know that school work is business and business always comes before recreation.
- ☐ I start my homework as soon after arriving home as possible.
- ☐ I tackle my hardest subject first, when at my freshest.
- ☐ I schedule my time, having an established homework routine that I stick to, though I keep it flexible in case something unexpected arises.
- ☐ I limit distractions once at work—no phone calls, TV, or music.
- ☐ I limit breaks to 15–30 minutes between *completed* assignments.
- ☐ I have a list of phone buddies to call when questions crop up or absences occur. (See next page)
- ☐ During the week, I see my friends only AFTER finishing my work.
- ☐ I always study out loud for tests, knowing that's the most effective way to learn. For test reviews, I make up possible test questions and answer them—both orally and in writing.
- ☐ I ask my parents and/or friends to quiz me only AFTER several independent review sessions.
- ☐ I always try to do and be my very best.

"No one will ever ask or expect you to do anything more than your very best. Do no less." ~ Carol Josel

PLANNING ON IT

"The only way to get a thing done is to start to do it. Then keep on doing it, and finally you'll finish it. You'll finish it, even if at first you thought you couldn't do it at all." ~ Langston Hughes

"Large tasks that seem overwhelming can be made very manageable by breaking them down into smaller tasks." ~ unknown

***BONUS TIPS:

♦ To succeed, take good notes.
♦ Do more than is required, such as attempting 12 math problems rather than just the 10 assigned. Remember that improvement comes with practice.
♦ Get in the study anywhere-everywhere habit—while on the bus, standing in line, eating lunch, etc.
♦ Post your vocabulary words on the bathroom mirror, learning a new word each time you wash up or brush your teeth.
♦ Make reading a bedtime ritual. Being well-read improves language sense, spelling skills, writing ability, grades, even conversations!

TIPS ALREADY IMPLEMENTED	TIPS THAT NEED DOING
1. _____	1. _____
2. _____	2. _____
3. _____	3. _____
4. _____	4. _____
5. _____	5. _____
6. _____	6. _____
7. _____	7. _____
8. _____	8. _____

"Homework builds the skills needed to cope with life." ~ Linda Sanna

"If you're coasting, you're going downhill." ~ J. T. Scully's dad

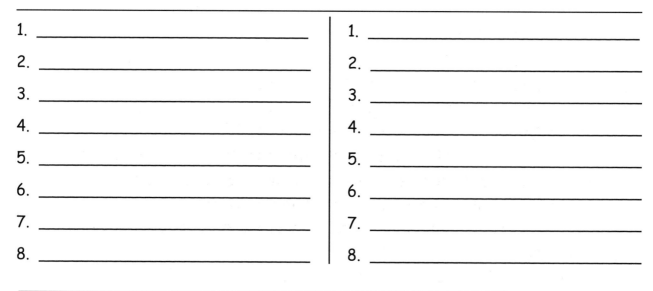

PHONE BUDDIES

Remember that your teachers will forge ahead whether you're in school or not, so, if you must be absent, be sure to call your friend(s) for missed assignments. Record their names and numbers below and post by your phone.

ENGLISH: _____

_____

EXPRESSIVE ARTS: _____

_____

HEALTH: _____

_____

FOREIGN LANGUAGE: _____

_____

MATH: _____

_____

READING: _____

_____

SCIENCE: _____

_____

SOCIAL STUDIES: _____

_____

Homework Helper Sites

To help you navigate through all those homework assignments and research papers, here are some highly regarded Internet sites to help you along your way:

- **Homework Central:** Instead of surfing, with just three clicks you're where you want to be. For example, Click one—History: United States; Click 2—1850-1856 Civil War Era; Click 3— Battles & Campaigns. www.homeworkheaven.com and HomeworkCentral.com

- **Studyweb:** This site offers 63,000 "research quality" links. More than 400 subject/topic pages take you to specific topics of interest. www. studyweb.com

- **Homework Help:** Hosted by the Minneapolis-St. Paul *Star Tribune*, this site offers six categories, including English, literature, social studies/civics. Submit homework questions and volunteer teachers e-mail back answers within 24 hours. New questions and answers are provided each week. No specific answers are given, only help in finding the answers. Here, you can also help fellow students with homework. www.startribune.com/education/

- **Ask Dr. Math:** Here, topics are organized by grade level using typical questions. If you can't find needed information, you can e-mail questions and receive a response in a few days. mathforum.org/dr.math

- **AOL's Homework Help & Ask-A-Teacher Services:** keyword is *homework*. More than 1,500 volunteer teachers answer about 8,000 e-mails a day from confused students.

- *Information Please:* A reference site containing an assortment of searchable almanacs, including one for students. www.infoplease.com

- *KidsClick!:* This site offers a searchable, comprehensive directory of Internet resources for students, selected by librarians, with notes on reading levels. www.kidsclick.org

- *No Sweat:* This site consists of Homework Central, Jr. for grades 1–6, Homework Central for grades 7 and up, and Encyclopedia Central for college and above. www.bigchalk.com

- *Middle School Cybrary:* This site offers Web resources for researching educational topics. An annotation accompanies each source which is then categorized for easy access to major topics. www.geocities.com/Athens/Academy/6617/

- *My Hero:* This is a great resource for researching the topic, *Heroes: People Who Made a Difference.* The site even has a section featuring teacher heroes. www.myhero.com

- *The Times Learning Network* brings world affairs to life for grade 6–12 teachers, students, and parents, all based on the news and archives of the *New York Times.* www.nytimes.com/learning

"Ninety percent of the information and knowledge required in the year 2000 was not even invented in 1990. Graduates will be exposed in 2000 to more information than their grandparents were exposed to in a lifetime."

~ Dr. Terrance Canning

VISIONS AND GOALS

"If you're not sure where you're going, you're likely to end somewhere else."
~ unknown

FIRST, list your most important responsibilities as a student:

1. _____   4. _____

2. _____   5. _____

3. _____   6. _____

NOW, scan the preceding pages, taking another look at all the suggestions recommended so far. Then highlight the most meaningful ones, choose your top eight, and record below:

1. _____   5. _____

2. _____   6. _____

3. _____   7. _____

4. _____   8. _____

FINALLY, couple your responsibilities and hopes with my suggestions, setting forth five short-term academic goals.

GOAL   TARGET DATE

1. _____   _____

2. _____   _____

3. _____   _____

4. _____   _____

5. _____

"If you have the courage to begin, you have the courage to succeed." ~ David Viscott

Part 3

TIME MANAGEMENT ACTIVITIES

WHERE AND WHEN SHOULD YOU STUDY?

DIRECTIONS: Check out each item below and indicate whether, in your view, it is a true or false statement.

_____ 1. As soon as possible after arriving home and enjoying a snack, you should start making a dent in your schoolwork.

_____ 2. Actually, the right time to start tackling schoolwork is right after dinner.

_____ 3. Ah, television. . . . It's best to save viewing for weekends, taping favorite shows during the week.

_____ 4. Actually, you should schedule your favorite television show right into your daily study schedule, even if you have "tons" of homework.

_____ 5. Listening to music while doing schoolwork enhances your concentration.

_____ 6. You need a specified study area in order to do your schoolwork effectively.

_____ 7. Advanced planning is not essential when deciding the order in which you'll tackle assignments. Just do it!

_____ 8. It's crazy to try to do any school-related work if you only have ten or fifteen minutes in which to do it.

9. Face it, students can't participate in extracurricular activities or enjoy friends and family and still succeed academically.

THE SCOOP ON WHERE AND WHEN

DIRECTIONS: Read the explanations that
follow and score yourself.

1. FALSE: Actually the answer depends primarily on the length of time you need to unwind from school. Most experts suggest starting in after a short break and a healthy snack, such as yogurt, fruit, and cheese. Avoid loading up on carbohydrates as they tend to make us sluggish. And keep in mind that most cans of soda contain about seven to ten teaspoons of sugar—even gingerale. Definitely to be avoided!

2. FALSE: Like number one, this item also depends on you. Just keep in mind that many of us grow weary after a long day and satisfying meal, so putting work off until after dinner may result in less than your best effort.

3. FALSE: Actually, you should schedule that favorite show right along with math, science, etc. Otherwise, you might just become resentful and produce less than quality work. Just keep it short and tape longer programming for weekend viewing.

4. TRUE: You know why now.

5. FALSE: Definitely! It's quite possible that a word or two of a song will end up in your essay. Perhaps this has already happened to you. But that's not the only problem with combining homework and music. Concentration demands a good deal of energy. If your mind must "tune out" distracting sounds while you're trying to study, you'll use up even more energy and tire twice as quickly!

6. FALSE: Some of us require a desk or table to work, while others find a bed or even the floor more conducive. Whatever your preference, just make sure you choose a quiet, no-traffic area equipped with good lighting. One student escaped her four younger siblings by retreating to her mom's closet. All she had to add was a pillow!

7. FALSE: There's only one option here, and that's to plan, leaving nothing to chance! Look over all your homework and upcoming tests, determine your hardest assignment and begin there, working your way through it all until ending with the easiest work. Remember that if you leave the most difficult assignments for last, you'll be too tired to give them the concentration they require.

8. FALSE: Short blocks of time are perfect for reviewing flash cards or notes, even organizing papers. Don't waste a minute if you can help it.

9. FALSE: As you'll soon discover, most of us don't realize how much time we actually waste and/or cannot account for. Remember that your goal should be finding a balance between school work, family, friends, extracurricular activities, and rest.

Scoring:
1-3 correct: Time to worry about time. Read on for recommendations and tips
4-6 correct: Your time management needs some fine-tuning. Tips follow.
7-9 correct: A bit of polishing and you'll be an ace manager of time.

TIME CONTROL: GETTING TO KNOW SAM

Directions: Take a careful look at Sam's schedule below and then answer the question that follows it.

6:30 – 7:30 a.m.	waking up, washing up, & eating breakfast
7:30 – 8:00 a.m.	waiting for bus & traveling to school
8:00 – 8:12 a.m.	homeroom
8:15 – 9:00 a.m.	1st Period
9:03 – 9:45 a.m.	2nd Period
9:48 – 10:33 a.m.	3rd period
10:36 – 11:21 a.m.	4th period
11:24 – 11:54 a.m.	lunch
11:57 – 12:42 p.m.	5th period
12:45 – 1:30 p.m.	6th period
1:33 – 2:18 p.m.	7th period
2:21 – 3:06 p.m.	8th period
3:06 – 3:30 p.m.	bus ride home
3:30 – 4:00 p.m.	change clothes, snack, phone calls
4:00 – 6:00 p.m.	play ball, watch TV, &/or play computer games
6:00 – 7:00 p.m.	eating dinner, washing dishes
7:00 – 8:00 p.m.	schoolwork
8:00 – 9:00 p.m.	TV watching
9:00 p.m.	bedtime

Sam says he's too busy to do more than one hour of homework a day. Hopefully, you disagree and can find at least two additional time slots, so that he could put in even 2-1/2 hours a day instead.

YOUR OWN SCHEDULE

DIRECTIONS: Now it's time to think about your own use of time, so let's get started. Following Sam's lead, complete your own typical school day schedule below, followed by your typical weekend schedule on the next page.

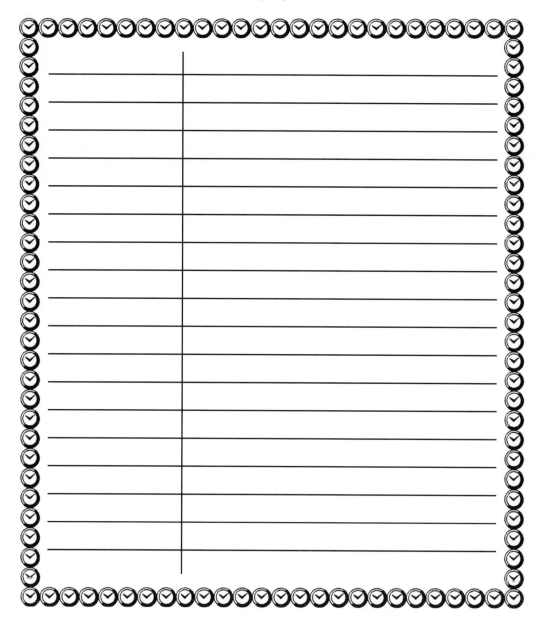

"Hold every moment sacred." ~ Thomas Mann

THE WEEKEND IS HERE!

What do your weekends look like? Are they filled with activities and chores or just lots of chilling out? In either case, chart your typical Saturday and Sunday on the schedule below, starting with your usual wake up call.

Saturday Times	Saturday Activities	Sunday Times	Sunday Activities

"Every morning in Africa, a gazelle wakes up. It knows it must run faster than the fastest lion or it will be killed. Every morning, a lion wakes up. It knows it must outrun the slowest gazelle or it will starve to death. It doesn't matter whether you are a lion or a gazelle; when the sun comes up, you'd better be running." ~ Successories

SAM'S 168

Study Sam's use-of-time chart below seeing how he allocates his time each day and week. Note that time is calculated in decimals:
.25 = 15 minutes (1/4 hour) .75 = 45 minutes (3/4 hour)
.50 = 30 minutes (1/2 hour) 1.00 = 60 minutes (1 hour)

ACTIVITY	PER DAY	PER WEEK
Transportation: To & From School	1.00 hour (2 x .50)	5 hours (5 x 1)
School	7.00 hours	35.0 hours (5 x 7)
Sleep	8.00 hours	56 hours (7 x 8)
Meals (.5 hours for each)	1.50 hours (3 x .50)	10.5 hours (7 x 1.5)
Homework & Studying	1.00 hour	5 hours (5 x 1)
Extracurricular Activities	1.50 hours	10.5 hours (7 x 1.5)
Job/Chores	.50 hours	3.5 hours (7 x .5)

	PER DAY	PER WEEK
TOTAL HOURS	20.50 hours	125.5 hours
UNACCOUNTED FOR HOURS	3.50 hours (24 –20.50)	**42.5 hours** (168-125.5)

Remember that Sam claims he has only about one hour a day for schoolwork—and none on the weekends, but he spends twice that amount on extracurricular activities! And, on top of all that, he can't account for more than 40 hours each week. That's more than an entire day and night, plus another day!!! What about you? Do you know where your time is flying off to? To find out, please turn the page.

YOUR 168

Eighth grader April Hunsberger defines time as opportunity flying by, and she might just be right about that. Most of us easily lose track of time, forever running out of it. Let's take a look at exactly where your time goes and how much of it you can't account for. To do so, fill in the table below, much the way Sam did on the previous page. Then calculate the hours you lose sight of every day and every week.

ACTIVITY	PER DAY	PER WEEK
Transportation: To & From School	(Going & returning)	(Per day # x 5)
School		(Per day # x 5)
Sleep		(Per day # x 7, plus extra weekend hours)
Meals (.5 hours for each)	(TIMES 3)	(Per day # x 7)
Homework & Studying		(Per day # x # of days it's done per week)
Extracurricular Activities		(Per day # x # of days so engaged per week)
Job/Chores		(Per day # x # of days so engaged per week)

TOTAL HOURS		
UNACCOUNTED FOR HOURS	(=24 – per day total)	(=168 – per week total)

TIMELY TIPS

DIRECTIONS: Do you Sometimes (S), Always (A), or Never (N) . . .

_____ 1. Create a daily TO-DO list?

_____ 2. Spend a *minimum* of 20 minutes per major subject each day?

_____ 3. Maintain a set study schedule, thus making homework a daily habit?

_____ 4. Engage in shorter study sessions for several days instead of a long cram session?

_____ 5. Tackle your hardest subjects first?

_____ 6. Take a short break AFTER each assignment is done, not in the middle of one?

_____ 7. Use breaks for phone calls, TV viewing, and/or enjoying a healthy snack, remembering to keep them short?

_____ 8. Guard against interruptions and distractions by unplugging the phone in your room if you have one, turning off lyric-containing music, and the like?

_____ 9. Take a short exercise break when too restless to settle down, so you can get your act together quickly?

_____10. Find a balance between your schoolwork, recreational activities, friends, and family? When are your free times? _____

_____

_____11. Prepare for the unexpected and adjust your schedule accordingly, and, if need be, revise it entirely?

_____12. Stack all school-related materials at your DROP SPOT when you have finished all your school work?

_____13. Aim for the same bedtime every night—and at a reasonable hour— so you'll be well-rested in the morning?

_____14. Make reading part of your bedtime ritual?

"Never say you don't have enough time. You have exactly the same number of hours per day as were given to Helen Keller, Albert Einstein, Michelangelo, Mother Teresa, and Leonardo da Vinci." ~ unknown

COUNT 'EM UP!

DIRECTIONS: Go back to the previous page, "Timely Tips," totaling your ALWAYS, SOMETIMES, NEVER responses, and then place your totals for each in the spaces provided below.

ALWAYS total: _____

SOMETIMES total: _____

NEVER total: _____

If you were able to answer with ALWAYS . . .

11 or more times: Very timely of you. Keep up the good work but keep trying to improve yourself, too.

7-10 times: Timely changes are needed to get you working at your best.

6 or less times: Make some timely moves now or you may never quite catch up.

TIMELY IMPROVEMENTS TO MAKE:

1. _____

2. _____

3. _____

4. _____

5. _____

6. _____

DAILY SCHEDULE

"Time is opportunity flying by." ~ April Hunsberger

MONDAY:

3:30 _____	5:30 _____	7:30 _____
4:00 _____	6:00 _____	8:00 _____
4:30 _____	6:30 _____	8:30 _____
5:00 _____	7:00 _____	9:00 _____

TUESDAY:

3:30 _____	5:30 _____	7:30 _____
4:00 _____	6:00 _____	8:00 _____
4:30 _____	6:30 _____	8:30 _____
5:00 _____	7:00 _____	9:00 _____

WEDNESDAY:

3:30 _____	5:30 _____	7:30 _____
4:00 _____	6:00 _____	8:00 _____
4:30 _____	6:30 _____	8:30 _____
5:00 _____	7:00 _____	9:00 _____

THURSDAY:

3:30 _____	5:30 _____	7:30 _____
4:00 _____	6:00 _____	8:00 _____
4:30 _____	6:30 _____	8:30 _____
5:00 _____	7:00 _____	9:00 _____

FRIDAY/WEEKEND:

3:30 _____	5:30 _____	7:30 _____
4:00 _____	6:00 _____	8:00 _____
4:30 _____	6:30 _____	8:30 _____
5:00 _____	7:00 _____	9:00 _____

Part 4

LEARNING STYLE ACTIVITIES

FINDING THE F's

DIRECTIONS: The following paragraph contains several F's. Your job is to count each one and then record your total number of F's on the space provided and cover immediately.

FINISHED FILES ARE THE
RESULT OF YEARS OF SCIENTIFIC
STUDY COMBINED WITH THE
EXPERIENCE OF MANY YEARS
OF EXPERTS.

My #: _____

As your classmates share their "F" number, jot them down below.

Not all those "F" numbers were identical, were they? How could they be? We all view and react to the world differently. We take in and recall information differently, as well. Turn the page to find your unique learning style.

FINDING YOURSELF:
THE VISUAL LEARNER

Directions: Check off the statements that apply to you and record your total below.

☐ Mind sometimes wanders, especially during lectures

☐ Observes rather than talks or acts

☐ Approaches tasks in an organized way

☐ Prefers to read silently

☐ Spells quite well

☐ Memorizes by "seeing" pictures

☐ Is not too distractible

☐ Has good handwriting

☐ Remembers faces better than names

☐ Recalls best what is seen rather than heard

☐ Prefers written or drawn instructions

☐ Finds verbal instructions difficult

☐ Plans ahead

☐ Often doodles

☐ Is fairly quiet by nature

☐ Dresses neatly

☐ Notices details

☐ Enjoys using computer graphics

☐ Likes putting puzzles together

☐ Does well creating maps, graphs, posters, charts, etc.

☐ Enjoys filmstrips and videos

When you finish finding yourself on this list, add up all your checkmarks and record your total score below: Your Score:

_____
20

FINDING YOURSELF:
THE AUDITORY LEARNER

DIRECTIONS: Check off the statements that apply to you and record your total below.

- ☐ Enjoys talking
- ☐ Often talks out loud to self
- ☐ Is quite easily distracted
- ☐ Has more difficulty with written directions
- ☐ Benefits from oral instructions
- ☐ Prefers to be read to rather than reading silently
- ☐ Whispers to self while silently reading
- ☐ Likes to read orally
- ☐ Enjoys choral readings
- ☐ Likes to listen to tape-recorded books
- ☐ Likes to ask and answer questions
- ☐ Enjoys debating and interviewing
- ☐ Learns best by listening and speaking
- ☐ Memorizes in steps, in a sequence
- ☐ Recalls best what is heard rather than seen
- ☐ Enjoys music
- ☐ Remembers names more than faces
- ☐ Is easily distracted by noise
- ☐ Often hums or sings
- ☐ Has an outgoing nature

When you finish finding yourself on this list, add up all your checkmarks and record your total below:

Your Score:

‾‾‾‾‾‾
20

FINDING YOURSELF:
THE KINESTHETIC LEARNER

DIRECTIONS: Check off the statements that apply to you and record your total below.

- ☐ Likes physical rewards
- ☐ Is often in motion
- ☐ Likes to touch people when talking to them
- ☐ Expresses emotions physically (hugging, etc.)
- ☐ Uses hands a good deal while talking
- ☐ Taps pencil or foot while studying
- ☐ Enjoys handling objects
- ☐ Does not give reading much priority
- ☐ Is essentially a poor speller
- ☐ Writing out directions is helpful
- ☐ Learns best by manipulating objects
- ☐ Easily recalls personal experiences
- ☐ Best follows directions that are performed or rehearsed
- ☐ Enjoys doing activities, such as science labs
- ☐ Best solves problems by physically working through them
- ☐ Enjoys building models and making dioramas
- ☐ Enjoys acting and role playing
- ☐ Likes to sketch and play board games
- ☐ Is willing to try new things
- ☐ Is outgoing by nature
- ☐ Dresses for comfort

When you finish finding yourself on this list, add up all your checkmarks and record your total below:

Your Score:

_____
20

SHARPENING THAT LEARNING STYLE

DIRECTIONS: Now you know that we learn, store, and recall information primarily by seeing, hearing, and touching, though to differing degrees. Determine your dominant modality by recording your scores from the preceding three pages below.

Visual Score: ____/20

Auditory Score: ____/20

Kinesthetic Score: ____/20

***If your scores are evenly divided between the three modalities, you are a more flexible learner, using a number of learning techniques depending on the task.

DIRECTIONS: Now use these suggested techniques to strengthen your dominant modality as well as the others.

VISUAL	AUDITORY	KINESTHETIC
• Form mental pictures • Take notes • Use parts of words to uncover and learn meanings • Use several notebooks • Color code materials • Use flash cards • Study graphs, charts, photos, charts, & maps • Use graphic organizers • Watch educational TV • Watch filmstrips and videos • Watch demonstrations • Draw • Use exhibits • Use a highlighter • Use mnemonics when memorizing (to follow)	• Use audiotapes • Watch educational TV • Make up rhymes & poems • Read information out loud • Repeat things orally • Engage in discussions • Listen carefully • Use oral directions • Sound out words • Say words in syllables • Copy carefully from the board/overhead • Watch alignment of math problems • Test yourself with a buddy or parent • Use a highlighter • Use mnemonics when memorizing (to follow)	• Pace/walk as you study • Physically enact information • Role play • Exercise • Write out information • Write on surfaces with your finger • Associate feelings with concepts, facts • Repeatedly write out lists of information • Move about often • Take frequent breaks • Use flash cards • Shut your eyes & write information in the air • Study with classical music softly playing • Use mnemonics when memorizing (to follow)

WHERE AND HOW YOU WORK

DIRECTIONS: Okay, we now know your learning style, but where and how do you go about working? To find out, circle your choices.

1. I'm sharpest in the MORNING, AFTERNOON, or NIGHT.

2. It has to be absolutely QUIET when I work; I like some BACKGROUND NOISE when I work.

3. I work best in DIM/BRIGHT lighting.

4. I SNACK/DON'T SNACK while doing schoolwork.

5. I work best at a DESK, on a BED, on the FLOOR.

6. I work best ALONE/WITH A FRIEND.

7. I work best where it's WARM/COOL.

"Self-confidence ultimately comes from accepting yourself and your decisions, regardless of what anybody else thinks or any mistakes you have made." ~ Albert Ellis, Ph.D.

Use this information to create your working profile on the next page . . .

MY WORKING PROFILE

BEST TIME TO STUDY: _____

BEST SOUND EFFECTS: _____

BEST LIGHTING: _____

BEST SNACK TIME: _____

BEST LOCATION: _____

BEST COMPANION: _____

BEST TEMPERATURE: _____

CHOOSE FROM THE FOLLOWING:

Morning	Dim	Bed
Afternoon	Bright	Floor
Evening	Right after school	Self
Quiet	During breaks	Friend
Background noise	While working	Warm
	Desk	Cool

Part 5

NOTE-TAKING ACTIVITIES

WHAT WAS THAT YOU JUST SAID???

DIRECTIONS: I want to get into your head and know your thoughts on NOTE-TAKING. That's right, note-taking. When a teacher tells you to put pencil to paper and record all the facts and figures s/he's about to share, what immediately crosses your mind? Here's your chance to tell all the good and the not-so-good when it comes to notes—and be ready to share.

1. _____

2. _____

3. _____

4. _____

5. _____

Now, I have a few questions for you to answer:

1. Have you ever had trouble keeping up with a lecturer? YES/NO

2. Do you like to lend your notes to classmates? YES/NO

3. Has anyone ever criticized your borrowed notes? YES/NO

4. Have you ever had trouble deciphering your own notes when you finally go over them? YES/NO

5. Have you ever interrupted a teacher because you missed an important piece of information? YES/NO

A NEW WAY OF LOOKING AT THINGS

DIRECTIONS: You're right. Note-taking has its problems—from writer's cramp and illegibility to critical classmates who borrow your notes—and then might just lose them! Meanwhile, teachers don't want to be interrupted for repeats and asking a neighbor puts you both behind. So what's a kid supposed to do? Don't despair. Remember that problems have solutions and help is on its way right now.

To begin, try deciphering these directions for writing a business letter. Just do your best and then read on. You're about to learn an abbreviated note-taking system that will soon have you keeping up with the fastest talker. Practice, though, is the key, so let's get started.

```
                              Bus. Ltr.

  1.  Hedng        = (on rt, 1" ← top) = add. & date
  2.  Insde Add. = (↓ 4-7 lnes)      = nme, titl, add.
  3.  Grting       = (↓ 2 lnes)        = Dear _____:
  4.  Bdy          = (↓ 2 lnes)        = indnt 5 spces each
  5.  Clsng        = (↓ 2 lnes)        = Sncrly,
  6.  Nme          = (↓ 4 lnes)        = Full nme (prntd)
  7.  Sig          = (b/tw #5 & 6)     = " " (cursve)
```

Your "translation" ~

1. _____

2. _____

3. _____

4. _____

5. _____

6. _____

7. _____

SO THAT'S WHAT IT SAID!

Okay, here's what those directions said, just so you know:

1. The address and date (heading) go on the right-hand side, one inch from the top of the paper.
2. Go down 4-7 lines and write the name, title, and address of the recipient (inside address).
3. Skip down two more lines and write your salutation (as in Dear Mr. Jones:).
4. Start the body, two lines down, indenting five spaces for each new paragraph.
5. Skip down two lines for the closing (as in Sincerely,).
6. Print your name in full four lines below the closing.
7. In between the closing and your printed name, write your signature.

How did you do? Did you come close or are you completely lost? Rate yourself below and then read on:

_____ I got most of it. (You're well on your way!)

_____ I figured out some of it. (Good for you!)

_____ I had no idea what this meant. (Be patient!)

Remember that this takes time and will take practice. Let's start with some note-taking tips and then we'll get more specific.

DID YOU KNOW THAT YOU SHOULD . . .

- Read about the topic in advance.
- Sit near the front of the room.
- Keep a "notes" section for each subject in your binder.
- Leave a wide left-hand margin for questions. (More on this to follow)
- Date & paginate each set of notes.
- Pretend the lecturer is speaking only to you. It will help keep you focused.
- Take notes on one side of paper only; leave the other side for added notes.
- Listen first; then write, jotting down only what you DON'T know.
- Listen for key words.
- Don't try to record every word.
- Don't write in complete sentences.
- Abbreviate as much as possible. (Short-cuts & abbreviations to follow)
- Indent to show relationships:
      Main points & definitions
            secondary points/supp. details
                  more subordinate information
- Write OB when something is on the board.
- Write R if an item is repeated.
- Write ** if told it's very important.
- Write EX for examples.
- Take special note of introductions and summaries.
- Leave blanks for missed information & ask a friend or teacher after class.
- Keep taking notes during discussions.
- Don't stop writing until class ends.
- That evening, "repair" notes, filling in blanks, improving legibility, etc.
- Use a highlighter to target important dates, facts, events, etc., as you review.
- Review notes several times a week— and always out loud.

Also listen for SIGNALS OF IMPORTANCE:

- Pauses
- Information that's repeated
- Slowed pacing
- A raised voice
- A lowered voice
- Information that's placed on the board or overhead
- Direct eye contact
- Dramatic gestures
- These and other similar phrases:
    "An important reason . . ."
    "The chief cause . . ."
    "Pay special attention to . . ."
    "Most importantly . . ."
    "First of all . . ."
    "To summarize . . ."
    "Therefore . . ."
    "As a result . . ."
    "On the other hand . . ."
    "The following causes, facts, reasons, effects, decisions . . ."
    and so on.

NOTE-TAKING SHORTCUTS

DIRECTIONS: Here's something to think about whenever you're about to say, "I don't have to write it down; I'll remember it!" Oh, really???

> *Within two weeks, you may forget as much as 80% of the information you heard today. After four weeks, you'll be lucky to remember even 5% of that information.*

In other words, the odds are against you, but help is on the way in the form of abbreviated note-taking. Take a good look at these suggested shortcuts and vow to practice using some of them right away.

A) Eliminate some vowels:
   If u cn rd ths, u can gt a gd jb.

B) Eliminate some unnecessary words, such as *a, an, the, this, that:*
   A fellow lifted the boulder. = Felo lfted boldr.

C) Substitute an = sign for verbs, especially linking verbs (*am, is, was, were, etc.*); it can sometimes take the place of *this* or *that*
   I am a teacher. = I = tchr.

D) Write just the beginnings of words, not the whole words:
   The Democrats and Republicans are our two political parties. = Dems & Reps = our 2 pol. prties.

E) Eliminate periods at the end of sentences. They'll just slow you down.

F) Code long/oft-repeated words in the margin: *P = photosynthesis*

G) Abbreviate frequently: → = *to;* ← = *from;* b/c = *because*
   (More samples follow on pages 78 & 79)

LET'S PRACTICE

DIRECTIONS: Try your hand at a bit of "translating," referring to the previous page for help.

(B = Beauregard)

1. Trn lft at crnr & trvl 2 blcks→Mn St = rt

_____

2. Stdy yr mth b4 Eng b/c mth exm = Tues, Eng. = Fri

_____

3. Tbls & chrs u ordrd = dlayd→Sat

_____

4. Pres. Jmes Grfld = sht at Wash. trn statn 7/2/1881

_____

5. 4/12/1861 = Genl. B = 1st shot on Ft. Smptr

_____

6. J. J. Astor = →Am ←Grmny & wrkd in NYC 4 $2/wk

_____

1. Turn left at the corner and travel two blocks to Main Street and make a right.
2. Study your math before English because the math exam is on Tuesday and the English one is on Friday.
3. The chairs you ordered have been delayed until Saturday.
4. President James Garfield was shot at a Washington train station on July 2, 1881.
5. On April 12, 1861, General Beauregard fired the first shot on Fort Sumpter.
6. John Jacob Astor came to America from Germany and worked in New York City for two dollars a week.

KEEP PRACTICING

How did you do with the previous page of translations?

_____ I was very successful   _____ I was somewhat successful

NOW, try your hand at "decoding" these definitions from various textbook glossaries. Each defined word has been left intact for you.
** Note that *w/ = with;* → *= to*

1. foreshadowing: use of clues in narr → sugg cmng action

_____

2. setting: tme & plce in whch evnts of stry tke plce

_____

3. clause: gr wrds w/ subj & v

_____

4. adverb: mdfies v, adj, or anthr adv & tlls hw, whn, whr, or → what xtnt

_____

5. tenement: aprtmnts mtng min stndrds

_____

6. patricians: powrfl up-clss cits of ancnt Rme

_____

7. oligarchy: govt = fw pepl rul

_____

8. classify: → grp idas, info, or obj bsed on thr sims

_____

KEEP GOING . . .

9. pathogen: any org = prod dsese

_____

10. balanced diet: fd etn drng dy tht gvs ur bdy nutrnts nded 4 lfe

_____

11. pentathlon: Olym gme w/ 5 evnts

_____

12. biennials: plnts = cmplet thr lfe cycl = 2 yrs

_____

13. speed: meas of hw far obj movs in gvn per of tme

_____

14. stratosphere: 2nd layr atmos

_____

15. mesa: hll hvng steep sdes & flt top

_____

1. foreshadowing = the use of clues in a narrative to suggest coming action
2. setting = the time and place in which events of a story take place
3. clause = a group of words with a subject and a verb
4. adverb = modifies verbs, adjectives, or another adverb and tells how, when, where, or to what extent
5. tenement = apartments meeting minimum standards
6. patricians = powerful upper-class citizens of ancient Rome
7. oligarchy = a government in which a few people rule
8. classify = to group ideas, information, or objects based on their similarities
9. pathogen = any organism that produces disease
10. balanced diet = food eaten during the day that gives your body the nutrients needed for life
11. pentathlon = Olympic game with five events
12. biennials = plants that complete their life cycle in two years
13. speed = a measure of how far an object moves in a given period of time
14. stratosphere = the second layer of the atmosphere
15. mesa = a hill having steep sides and a flat top

HOW DID YOU DO?? _____ very good _____ good _____ not so good

NOW, GET THOSE ABBS WORKING!

More practice sessions will follow. For now, let's add to your "personal shorthand." Many of these abbreviations may already be familiar to you, so just highlight those that are not. Note that most simply represent first syllables—and there's no end to the possibilities.

meas = measure (-ment)	org = organize; organization
rep = represent	sugg = suggest(-ed) (-ion)
wk = week	min = minimum
wknd = weekend	max = maximum
punc = punctuation	combo = combination
gen'l = general	sig = significant
mins = minutes	obj = object
secs = seconds	subj = subject
ex = example	attn = attention
imp = important	etc. = etcetera; and so on
cits = citizens	bio = biology
vocab = vocabulary	Eng = English, England
info = information	ss = social studies
def = definition	sci = science
cap = capital; capitol	rdg = reading
caps = capitals	Fr; Sp = French; Spanish

ANOTHER KIND OF ABB WORKOUT

These abbreviations rely mostly on symbols. Adding them to your "shorthand" will further speed you on your note-taking way. Highlight unfamiliar ones and begin incorporating them right away!

→ = to, resulting in	° = degree
← = from, as a result of	R = right (L = left)
↑ = up, upward; increase (-ing)	@ = at; around
↓ = down (-ward);, increase (-ing)	¶ = paragraph
$ = money; dollars; currency	** = important information
¢ = cents	> = more than
1st/2nd . . . = first, second, & so on	< = less than
b/tw = between	≯ = not more than
re: = regarding; about	≮ = not less than
w/ = with	x = times (as in 2x)
w/o = without	÷ = divided by; (= dividers)
?'s = questions	= = equal (-s)
: = following; to follow	≠ = not equal to
/ = or (as in *pencil/pen*)	⊥ = perpendicular
# = number (#'s = numbers)	‖ = parallel
" = inches; ditto	∴ = therefore
' = foot; feet; apostrophe	H_2O = water

EXERCISING ALL THOSE ABBS

DIRECTIONS: Here's your chance to put to the test all you're learning about abbreviating, as you try your hand with these subject-area rules and definitions. Take your time and do your best. Refer back to previous pages when in doubt as to a symbol or shortcut. Then "Check It Out" on page 82.

1. contractions: use an apostrophe to show where letters, numbers, or words have been omitted in a contraction

_____

2. median: the middle number in a group of numbers when the numbers are listed in order

_____

3. mixed number: a number that has a whole number part and a fraction part

_____

4. acute angle: an angle with a measure less than 90 degrees

_____

5. obtuse angle: an angle with a measure more than 90 degrees and less than 180 degrees

_____

6. inflation: period when prices go up and money value goes down

_____

7. Manifest Destiny: the belief that the United States should extend from coast to coast

_____

8. plebians: poor and lower-class citizens of ancient Rome

_____

KEEP GOING . . .

DIRECTIONS: This time, you'll try your hand at "translating" these already abbreviated textbook definitions. Refer back to previous pages when in doubt as to a symbol or short-cut.

1. innate behavior: bhavr org = born w/ & lernd

_____

2. clone: ind. = gneticly = → 1 of parnts

_____

3. saliva: H_2Ory subst prod in mouth tht bgns chem dig of fd

_____

4. annuals: plnts = grw ← sds, prod sds, & die = 1 yr

_____

5. atmospheric pressure: meas of wt of air mols prssng ↓ on spec pt on Erth

_____

6. hail: H_2O drplts = frez in lyrs @ sm ice nucleus

_____

7. over-the-counter drugs: meds = purch w/o dr's rx

_____

8. science: knwldg all fcts knwn re: wrld & meths used → lrn/expln thse fcts

_____

CHECK IT OUT

DIRECTIONS: Compare your work with these possibilities and then assess your progress below.

EXERCISING ALL THOSE ABBS:
1. contractions: use ', shw whr ltrs/#'s/wrds = omttd in contr →
2. median: mid # in grp of #'s whn #'s = lstd in ordr
3. mixed number: ∟ # w/ whle # prt & frac prt
4. acute angle: ∟ w/ meas < 90°
5. obtuse angle: w/ meas > 90° & < 180°
6. inflation: per whn prces = ↓ & $ valu = ↑
7. Manifest Destiny: blef = US shud xtnd → coast → coast ← coast
8. plebians: poor & ↑-clss cits of anc. Rme

KEEP GOING:
1. innate behavior: the behavior an organism is born with and is not learned
2. clone: an individual genetically identical to one of its parents
3. saliva: the watery substance produced in the mouth that begins the chemical diges-tion of food
4. annuals: plants that grow from seeds, produce seeds, and die in one year
5. atmospheric pressure: the measure of the weight of the air molecules pressing down on a specific point on the Earth
6. hail: water droplets that freeze in layers around a small ice nucleus
7. over-the-counter drugs: medications that are purchased without a doctor's prescription
8. science: the knowledge of all the facts known about the world and the methods used to learn and explain those facts

---

NOW, HOW DO YOU GRADE YOURSELF? A B C D (circle one)

Strengths: _____

_____

_____

Weaknesses: _____

_____

_____

ABBREVIATE! ABBREVIATE!

DIRECTIONS: Abbreviate this description of the Battle of Bunker Hill as much as you possibly can, using every short-cut imaginable, including a code for often used longer words/names.

The Battle of Bunker Hill: It was June 16th, and the Americans had occupied both Bunker Hill and Breed's Hill. These were two high points near Charles Town, across the harbor from Boston. They worked all night and finally managed to build a *redoubt*, or earthen fort, on Breed's Hill. The very next day, on June 17th, Major General William Howe and 1,500 Redcoats crossed the bay, prepared to fight. Howe led one force around the base of Breed's Hill to attack from the rear. Brigadier General Robert Pigot led the rest of the Redcoats straight up the hill in three broad lines.

The Americans were tired and hungry, and fresh troops never came to relieve them. But their commander, Colonel William Prescott, kept their spirits up, supposedly telling them, "Don't fire till you see the whites of their eyes!" When the Redcoats were almost to the wall of the redoubt, the Americans finally fired back, sending the Redcoats back down the hill. They did the same thing to Howe and his men. Regrouping, the two commanders sent their Redcoats back up the hill a second time, and again the Americans turned them back. But then fresh British troops arrived, and, as they attacked for the third time, the Americans ran out of ammunition and finally had to give up this high ground to the British. In the end more than 1,000 Redcoats died or were wounded; about 100 Americans lost their lives, while another 300 were either wounded or taken prisoner, in what has come to be known as the Battle of Bunker Hill.

ONE WAY OF LOOKING AT IT

DIRECTIONS: Here is one way of abbreviating the description of the Battle of Bunker Hill. Note all the symbols and other short-cuts, including omitted words. Then make your comparisons. How can you improve your own abbreviating? Does most of this make sense to you?

Battle of Bunker Hill:
(B = Bunker Hill) (Br's = Breed's Hill)
(R's = Redcoats) (H= Howe) (P = Pigot)

6/16: Ams occ B & Br's Hlls nr Ch Twn, acrs hrbr ← Bstn. Wrkd all nite = redout (erthn frt) on Br's.

6/17: Maj Genl H & 1500 R's crss bay → Br's. & H w/ 1 frce = @ base → attck rear. Brig Genl P & rst of R's = ↑ hll in 3 lns.

Ams. = tird & hngry; no frsh troops. Ledr = Col Wm Prscott keps sprits ↑ = "No fire → see whtes of eys." Ams fire whn P & R's almst → wall & snd R's bck ↓. " for H & his men.

H & P regrp & = ↑ hll = 2nd tme & agan snt bck ↓.

Now, w/ frsh troops, R's = ↑ 4 3rd tme; Ams = no mre ammo & gve ↑.

In end: 1000 R's = ded/wunded; 100 Ams = ded & 300 wunded/imprsond.

NOW, DECIDE:

_____   This mostly makes sense to me.

_____   I need to practice a lot more! (Actually, many of us do!)

84

YOUR TURN

DIRECTIONS: Find a paragraph from one of your textbooks and abbreviate it as well and as much as you can. Then give it to a classmate to "translate." Remember to be careful not to omit too much.

_____

_____

_____

_____

_____

_____

_____

_____

_____

_____

_____

_____

_____

_____

_____

_____

_____

Text Title: _____ page # _____

Part 6

STUDY SKILL
ACTIVITIES

TACKLING SCHOOLWORK

DIRECTIONS: Check off all items that pertain to you.

- ☐ The only skimming of a text chapter I do is to count the number of pages I have to read.
- ☐ I put off doing schoolwork for as long as I can.
- ☐ My mind wanders when I'm reading a chapter.
- ☐ I'm a last minute kind of person when it comes to test preparation.
- ☐ I'll read a chapter as quickly as I can to get it done.
- ☐ My mom/dad has to make me sit down to do my work.
- ☐ I don't always think about what I'm reading; I just do it!
- ☐ I love the pages loaded with pictures, etc. It means less reading for me, and I barely glance at them.
- ☐ I mark the end of the chapter ahead of time so I can keep track of how much is left from time to time.
- ☐ I usually can't remember what I just read.
- ☐ I panic during tests, forgetting much of what I studied the night before.
- ☐ I rarely review my notes.
- ☐ Once I've read a chapter, I have to hunt for answers to end-of-chapter questions.
- ☐ To prepare for a test, I usually read the chapter(s) again.
- ☐ To prepare for a test, I sometimes reread a chapter more than once.
- ☐ I seldom if ever study out loud for a test.

My grand total of check marks is _____

WHAT IT MEANS: Each item represents a problem for you when it comes to schoolwork. Each also represents a solution. Recognizing the problem is the first step to improvement. It only takes 21 days to change a habit! Only one person can make a difference in your life, and that's you. Read on to make that difference, to change your habits and the way you approach schoolwork.

GETTING STARTED

You now know that . . .

- you need a quiet place in which to work
- an organized, well-supplied work space is essential
- a flexible schedule is a daily must
- schoolwork comes first and deserves about two hours a day of your attention
- you should tackle your hardest subject(s) first

Now, you're ready to study, BUT HOW? To start, answer these questions—without peeking at your text!

1. You know the copyright date of your text. YES/NO
2. You know if end-of-chapter questions are provided. YES/NO
3. You know if the authors provided end-of-chapter reviews. YES/NO
4. You know if summaries conclude each chapter section. YES/NO
5. You know if there's a subject index. YES/NO
6. You know if terms are **boldfaced** or *italicized*. YES/NO
7. You know if the text contains an appendix. YES/NO
8. If there is one, you know what information is contained in the appendix. YES/NO

*** Said "No" more than once? Let's get to work!

A MAN NAMED ROBINSON

His name was Francis Robinson, Dr. Francis Robinson to be exact—a psychologist at Ohio State University. The year was 1941 when his *Effective Reading* was published, and legend has it that he had his daughter in mind when he wrote it. She was a seventh grader at the time—and not a very successful one, or so the story goes. This, of course, worried the good professor, and he spent long nights figuring out a way to help her be a better student. And so his now famous SQ3R was born—a tried and true, classic approach to reading text and preparing for tests. It is said that it dramatically improved his daughter's grades as it has countless other children—and it can do the same for you.

That "**S**" stands for **survey**, so let's follow Robinson's advice and begin by surveying one of your textbooks:

1. Check out the TITLE PAGE and tell me the:

    Title: _____

    Author: _____ Copyright date: _____

    Why do you think it's important to know the copyright date?

    _____

    _____

2. If included, the INTRODUCTION or PREFACE will be found in the beginning of the text. This is a special message from the author(s) telling a bit about the information in the book, how it is organized, and how it will help you understand the subject better. List two things explained about your text in the introduction/preface—if there is one.

    a) _____

    b) _____

KEEP ON SURVEYING

3. The TABLE OF CONTENTS offers a glimpse at the special features of the text, the types of information provided, and how that information is arranged. It usually follows the Title Page, with chapters grouped under major headings. Please list the major headings of the first four units.

    a) _____   c) _____
    b) _____   d) _____

4. A GLOSSARY (dictionary of technical terms) is probably located in the back of your textbook. Take a look and estimate how many words you're familiar with: <25% <50% <75%. Here's an example:

    Graph: A drawing used to show information in an organized way.
    Greatest common factor: 1) The greatest number that is a factor of two or more numbers. 2) The greatest number that divides two or more numbers with no remainder.
    Greatest possible error: One half of the unit being used to find a measure.

5. Are technical terms **boldfaced** or *italicized* in this book? (Circle one).

6. The SUBJECT INDEX, like the sample below, also appears at the end of the text and is an alphabetical listing of the names, places, and subjects referred to in the book along with their page numbers:

    Equal Rights Amendment, 689
    Ericson, Leif, 12, 13, 14
    Eric the Red, 12
    Erie Canal, 292, 293, 308, 346
    Erie, Lake, 297-298
    Eskimo, 5, 168

    How complete does your INDEX appear to be? **Very/Not Very**

7. The APPENDIX, also found toward the end, is made up of additional materials and information of interest, such as maps, the Periodic Table, and the Constitution. What, if any, information is provided in your text's appendix?

    a) _____   c) _____
    b) _____   d) _____

CHAPTER SURVEYING

DIRECTIONS: *Select a chapter and answer these questions.*

1. Chapter title: _____ # of pages: _____

2. Now quickly read the introductory and concluding paragraphs.

3. What do you already know about this topic?_____
   _____

4. What do you hope to learn from the author? _____
   _____

5. About how long will it take to read? _____

6. List the first four (4) major headings of this chapter:
   a) _____   c) _____
   b) _____   d) _____

7. SUMMARIES pull together main ideas in each section and/or the entire chapter. Reading them first establishes a mind-set before you read about the topic in detail. Read the summary(ies) and list three main ideas covered in your chapter.
   a) _____
   b) _____
   c) _____

8. Circle the graphic aids found in this chapter & read their captions:
   graphs   maps   tables/charts   photos   drawings   diagrams

9. Now read the end-of chapter questions and review materials. What specific review activities are provided?

   _____

   _____

*** In one study, 1,500 Harvard students were given 2 hours to read a social studies chapter. After 22 minutes, the students were interrupted & asked to briefly describe what the chapter was about. Only 150 had surveyed the chapter. Most simply started reading, while many who looked ahead only did so to figure the length of the assignment. Only 15 (1%) could provide a general description of where the chapter was going. Everyone else "failed" to carefully survey.

THE ALL-IMPORTANT "Q"

Once a chapter has been surveyed and a mind-set has been established regarding the topic, the next step is to jot down questions in a two-column format. In this way, you'll be creating study guides that will make studying a breeze—even for final exams! Who wants to reread a chapter, let alone an entire text? Well, you'll NEVER have to do it again when you follow these steps:

1. Fold your paper lengthwise to leave a **wide, left-hand** margin. This is where you'll jot down all those questions—in very abbreviated form.
2. Use WHO, WHAT, WHERE, WHEN, WHY, or HOW to turn headings and sub-headings into questions. (A practice session follows)
3. Do the same thing with main ideas, which you'll usually find in the first or last sentence of textbook paragraphs.
4. Jot down end-of-chapter questions, too.

LET'S PRACTICE: Turn these headings into questions—abbreviated questions.

For example: *The Stamp Act* becomes *What = Stmp Act?* (This can be further abbreviated by simply writing, *Stmp Act?*)

1. The Boston Massacre = _____

2. The Goths and the Vandals = _____

3. The Decline of the Empire = _____

4. Fossil Fuels = _____

5. Soil Types = _____

SAMPLE TWO-COLUMN NOTES

DIRECTIONS: Notice how these notes about Pennsylvania and Philadelphia are set up and then try to decipher them.

PA?	1. gft ← Kng Ch II → Wm Penn → pay dad's (Adm. Pnn) debt 2. = safe hme 4 Quakrs 3. = Pnn's Frest (aftr Dad) 4. = brdrs: NJ, NY, MD
Phila?	1. = cty of bro luv 2. = 1st plnnd town in Am w/chkr-bord st. pttrn

Here's what all of that said:

Pennsylvania was a gift from King Charles II to William Penn as a way to pay the debt owed to his father, Admiral Penn. It established a safe home for the Quakers and means Penn's Forest, after Admiral Penn. Pennsylvania borders on New Jersey, New York, and Maryland.

Philadelphia is known as the city of brotherly love and was the first planned town in America, with its checker-board street pattern.

Are you with me? Remember to practice abbreviating every chance you get to perfect your own note-taking!

LAST STEPS

It is a well-known fact that students who have some idea of what they are going to read understand more of what they read. They have a framework into which new information can be stored. That's why SURVEYING is so important.

And having QUESTIONS firmly in place before reading an assignment gives you a reason to read—you're looking for answers! No more mindless page-turning and forgetting. You're hunting; you're writing; you're actively engaged in learning.

That, of course, means we've reached those three R's, the first of which is READ. Robinson wants you to first look over all your questions so you'll be mindful of them as you read and search for answers. As you find them, jot them down in an abbreviated, two-column format and, voilá, you've created a study guide! No more daydreaming or re-readings! (Use flash cards, too, especially for memorizing definitions, dates, and events.)

The fourth step is to RECITE. Robinson wants you talking your way through your notes, teaching the pillow, so to speak. To the senses of sight (reading) and touch (writing), you now add sound, insuring that information will be remembered—for a long time! Fold your paper so that you can only see your questions, and then ask each one of them in turn. When uncertain about an answer, just flip the paper over. Then test yourself again, asking the same question. Parents and/or friends can also test you once you feel confident enough.

The final step is to REVIEW. Repetition is a powerful memory aid. Reciting your notes a few times a week guarantees learning and retention. That's something cramming will never do for you!   LET'S TRY IT!

REASONS FOR MOVING WEST

From *Many Americans—One Nation*

DIRECTIONS: As you read this page, follow Robinson's prescription: quickly survey, jot down questions on the following page (pulled from headings, sub-headings, and/or topic sentences), read to find the answers, and record these beside their questions. Like a teacher, pull only important ideas from the text. DO NOT make note of what you already know!

There were many reasons why people moved west. Some, like Daniel Boone, were moved by the spirit of adventure. But most of the pioneers were looking for new lands to settle and farm.

Many pioneers had come to America because they had heard it was the "promised land." But when they got here, they found that all the good land along the coast was taken. For them, the West was the only answer. A traveler on the Wilderness Road gives us a description of the journey:

> Women and children in the month of December traveled a wilderness through ice and snow, passing large rivers and creeks, without shoe or stocking, and barely as many rags as covers their nakedness. . . . Here are hundreds traveling hundreds of miles, they know not what for nor where, except it's to Kentucky . . . The Promised Land . . . The Land of Milk and Honey.

Other settlers moved west in search of better land. What was wrong with the land they already had? A European visitor to the colonies described it this way:

> Agriculture was in a very bad state here. When a person had bought a piece of land, he cut down part of the woods, tore up the roots, plowed the ground, planted corn on it, and got a good crop the first year. But the same land, after several years of not being fertilized, loses its richness. Its owner then leaves it unplanted and moves to another part of his land, which he treats the same way. And so he goes on until he has changed a great part of his land into cornfields and has used up the richness of his soil. (Goldshlag, pp. 149–150)

TWO-COLUMN PRACTICE

Text: _The Free and the Brave_   Name: _____

Page: <u>58</u>   Date: _____

QUESTIONS TO ANSWER:

1. Did you pull your question from the heading? YES/NO
2. Did you abbreviate all your notes? YES/NO
3. Did you put your answer in list form since you were citing reasons for the westward movement? YES/NO
4. Did you leave out unnecessary details? YES/NO
5. Did you leave out information you already knew? YES/NO

Answered YES five times?   Superior note-taking!
Answered YES four times?   Good for you!
Answered less than that?   Keep at it, & you'll soon be a pro!

Part 7

MEMORY TECHNIQUE ACTIVITIES

YOUR SQ3R CHECKLIST

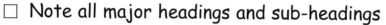

SURVEY:
☐ Note all major headings and sub-headings
☐ Look over all pictures, maps, charts, graphs, & captions
☐ Read first and last sentence of each paragraph
☐ Read the summary at the end of sections & the chapter
☐ Look over end-of-chapter questions

QUESTION:
☐ Leave a wide left-hand margin for recording questions
☐ Use WHO, WHAT, WHERE, WHEN, WHY, or HOW to turn head ings and sub-headings into questions
☐ Ditto for main ideas (usually first or last sentence in a textbook paragraph)
☐ Jot down end-of-chapter questions
☐ Create flash cards for **boldfaced**/*italicized* vocabulary

READ:
☐ Read over all of the questions you've jotted down
☐ As you read and find the answers, write them down beside the ap- propriate questions, creating a two-column study guide

RECITE:
☐ Ask and answer your questions out loud, looking back when unsure of an answer

REVIEW:
☐ Never cram for tests
☐ Go over your two-column notes a few times a week

A TRUE STORY

Time seemed to stand still, as she sat hunched in front of her computer, fingers flying over the keyboard. Fact after carefully researched fact about Ellis Island and the immigrants who passed through it made their way onto the screen. The paper was practically writing itself—on page eight already! And then the phone rang.

Wanting privacy, she abandoned her computer for a few minutes to take the call in her bedroom down the hall. Meanwhile, her mom, stir-frying chicken and vegetables down in the kitchen, decided to run upstairs for a sweater. Spotting that a light had been left on in the computer room, she flicked the switch, grabbed a sweater, and went back to her cooking. Such a howl!! Eight pages typed but UNSAVED, all gone with a flick of a switch! No saving to a disk or hard drive. You would howl too! Eight pages . . .

Like a computer, our minds are equipped with two basic types of memory—one will let you down more often than not. Our working, or short-term, memory allows us to keep a thought—but not for long! Quite simply, it's erased! Storing information, on the other hand, is our long-term memory's job; think of it as your personal hard drive. To prove the point, do this:

1. Grab a phone book and look up an unfamiliar number—a florist, physician, pharmacist, moving company, pizza man, . . .
2. Glance at the number, close the phone book, and dial the number.
3. Quickly hang up—we're not ordering anything today.
4. Now talk to someone for a few minutes—if need be, yourself!
5. Dial that same number again. Can you? Probably not! That number faded from your working memory as surely as if someone had flicked a light switch! (Ever forget your own phone number!!??)

MORAL OF THE STORY: Forgetting will occur. Count on it and then do something about it. To learn how, read on . . .

DIAL AWAY!

DIRECTIONS: Just in case dialing that florist or whomever didn't convince you that your working memory's other name is SHORT-TERM, here's another opportunity. Fill in the squares below as if they were the buttons on your phone—you know, that device you use just about every day. I want all the numbers, letters, and symbols in their correct position.

MEMORY LESSON #1: Repetition is good, but only if it is coupled with the intention to learn and remember. This is known as "focused repetition." We dial up all the time—but not mindfully!!!

MEMORY LESSON #2: This one you already know: *always* study and/or review OUT LOUD. Recitation is the most powerful learning tool around! Be your own teacher by **writing** and **reciting**, thus using all your senses. The results will amaze you!

UH, OH!

Think of this story as a reminder. It's one my professor shared with me, and now I'll share it with you. He said that if I leave all my studying for the night before a test—cramming—I'll probably go to bed feeling pretty confident, feeling like I'm ready for anything tomorrow's test will throw at me. All that information is now stuffed into my brain, so good night, sleep tight. But then comes the dawn, and I'll notice that a couple of facts have slipped my mind as if they had "leaked" out of my brain. And they have by as much as 10%—and I'm not even dressed yet!

Now, here's a new word for you: *interference*. Think of it as anything that distracts us from remembering or learning something in the first place. Perhaps I listened to the Beatles while I studied, or, on test day, I overslept and skipped breakfast, mom scolded me, my best friend is mad at me, and I have to sit through three classes before I get to take my test. INTERFERENCE!!!

The end: According to Professor Pedlow, distractions will continually pile up, and because that information was never "saved" in my long-term memory, it will soon fade. In two weeks, I'll only recall about 20% of it; in a month, I'll probably be down to only 5%. Yikes!

So there it is. Memories fade and brains have minds of their own. To appreciate that last bit of information, complete this little ditty; then we'll get back to solving our forgetfulness.

Question: What do you call the tree that grows from an acorn?
Answer: Oak
Question: What do you call a funny story?
Answer: Joke
Question: What do you call the sound a frog makes?
Answer: Croak
Question: What do you call the white of an egg?
Answer: _____

Check with your teacher and mark the correct statement:
___ I got it right!   ___ Oops! My brain really does have a mind of its own!

Cool brain facts follow:

BRAINY FACTS

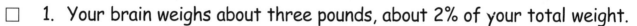

DIRECTIONS: Check off each brainy fact you already know.

☐ 1. Your brain weighs about three pounds, about 2% of your total weight.

☐ 2. Your brain uses 20-25% of your body's energy.

☐ 3. A computer with the same capacity as your brain would be 100 stories tall and cover the entire state of Texas.

☐ 4. Thinking is as tiring as physical labor.

☐ 5. Several billion bits of information pass through your brain every second.

☐ 6. Messages in your brain travel through its neural connections at speeds up to 250 miles per hour.

☐ 7. Your brain generates 25 watts of power while you're awake—enough to illuminate a light bulb.

☐ 8. Blueberries and spinach leaves are brain foods.

☐ 9. The brain may have its own "funny bone." Located in a small part of the frontal lobe, it enables us to appreciate jokes.

☐ 10. Experts claim we use only 1%, 2%, 5%, or 10% of our brain's capacity. It just depends on which expert's opinion you choose to believe.

> "If you're kind of tired . . . you can't pay attention well enough to remember things." ~ Douglas J. Hermann, Ph.D.

Add up your check marks & score yourself: _____/10 or _____%.

"Rats eating a diet rich in extracts from blueberries, strawberries, and spinach (full of cell-saving antioxidants) scored better on memory tests than those who did not." ~ SELF Magazine

Read on to become more brain-wise . . .

INFORMATION OVERLOAD

A page of vocabulary words and definitions, long lists of dates accompanied by their dates, reams of notes—unless they're of the two-column variety, and your brain will swoon. It's just too much information to handle in one bite, so to speak.

TRY THIS: In 30 seconds, memorize these numbers in order. *Go!!!*

1 4 9 2 1 9 8 4 1 7 7 6 1 8 1 2

Okay, time's up. Cover up and test yourself.
No peeking!

Here is some more practice for you, but this time group the numbers in some way (as in the dates 1492, etc.). Again, give yourself 30 seconds, cover up, and test. *Go!!!*

1 8 0 8 5 3 6 1 2 7 7 4 9 2

1 0 2 7 3 5 9 2 3 7 1 4 2 0

9 1 7 6 2 1 6 4 6 4 0 9 8

MEMORY LESSON #3: This grouping of information is often referred to as "chunking" and is particularly helpful in the rote memorization of facts, dates, formulas, definitions, and the like. That's why flash cards are so helpful. As you go through them, sort into two piles: those you're sure of and those you're not. Focus on those shaky ones. Once you feel confident that you know them all, test yourself on the entire stack again.

P.S. Think about it: Even the phone company understands this idea of chunking. Instead of seeing a number such as 12345678912, you'll see it listed as: 1-234-567-8912. Now it's all grouped for learning!

REMEMBER THIS!

"Our brains are able to accept 10 new facts every second!!!"

DIRECTIONS: Here's another chance to flex your brain power and prove a point too. In ONE minute, memorize all twenty of these words—in any order. *GO!!!*

tall, orange, French, comedy, apple, thin, strawberry, opera, fat, pear, English, drama, pretty, history, ballet, chemistry, short, algebra, circus, grape

YOUR MINUTE IS UP! COVER UP & TEST YOURSELF.

1. _____
2. _____
3. _____
4. _____
5. _____
6. _____
7. _____
8. _____
9. _____
10. _____

11. _____
12. _____
13. _____
14. _____
15. _____
16. _____
17. _____
18. _____
19. _____
20. _____

\# of words recalled: _____
Your score: _____/20 = _____%

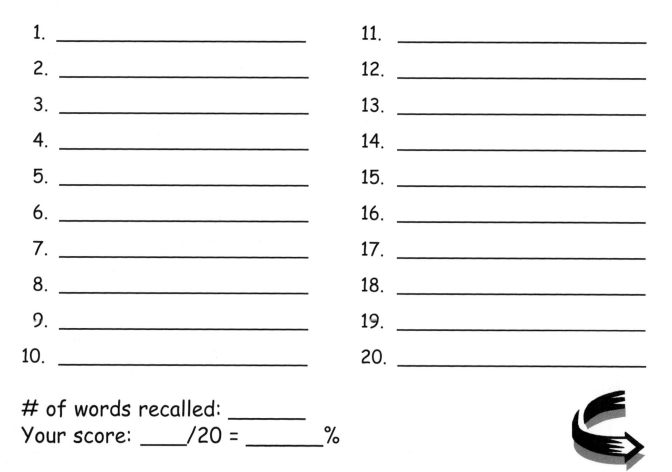

CHUNK IT!

Following Ma Bell's lead, those same twenty words are duplicated here, but this time they are grouped by categories from the physical to school subjects, fruits, and forms of entertainment. Again, you have one minute to memorize them in any order. *GO!!!*

tall	English	orange	comedy
thin	French	apple	ballet
fat	history	strawberry	drama
short	chemistry	pear	opera
pretty	algebra	grape	circus

1. _____
2. _____
3. _____
4. _____
5. _____
6. _____
7. _____
8. _____
9. _____
10. _____

11. _____
12. _____
13. _____
14. _____
15. _____
16. _____
17. _____
18. _____
19. _____
20. _____

\# of words recalled: _____

Your score: _____/20 = _____%

I did better this time: **Yes? No?**

(Most people improve significantly, thanks to chunking. DO IT!)

> *"The true art of memory is the art of attention."* ~ *Samuel Johnson*

MEMORY GAMES

DIRECTIONS: You have two minutes to memorize the following:

1. The planets IN ORDER, moving away from the sun:

   Mercury, Venus, Earth, Mars, Jupiter, Saturn, Uranus, Neptune, Pluto

2. The colors of the visible spectrum IN ORDER as they appear:

   red, orange, yellow, green, blue, indigo, violet

3. The spellings of these words:

   veterinarian   familiar   advantageous   niece

YOUR TWO MINUTES ARE UP! Cover up and be tested.

Planets: 1. _____   2. _____   3. _____

4. _____   5. _____   6. _____

7. _____   8. _____   9. _____

Spectrum: 10. _____   11. _____   12. _____   13. _____

14. _____   15. _____   16. _____

Spelling: 17. _____   18. _____

19. _____   20. _____

HOW DID YOU DO? ____/20 = ____%

MEMORY REMEDIES

DIRECTIONS: Check out these solutions. Try them on for size and start applying them every time you give your memory a workout.

1. SENTENCE CUES: Using the first letter of each item to be memorized, create a sentence (or two or three . . .)—the sillier the better! Here's your sentence cue for the nine planets:

<u>M</u>y <u>V</u>ery <u>E</u>legant <u>M</u>other <u>J</u>ust <u>S</u>erved <u>U</u>s <u>N</u>ine <u>P</u>izzas

2. ACRONYMS: Using the first letter or two of each item to be memorized, create a new word(s). Here's your acronym for the colors of the visible spectrum:

ROY G. BIV

3. SPELLING MNEMONICS: Look for word(s) within the word to be learned and create a memory jogger for the tricky spot(s), such as the following mnemonic sentences:

veter<u>in</u>arian:	Erin wants to be a veter<u>in</u>arian.
famil<u>iar</u>:	You are a famil<u>iar</u> <u>liar</u>.
advant<u>age</u>ous:	It's advant<u>age</u>ous to <u>age</u>.
n<u>ie</u>ce:	My n<u>ie</u>ce loves p<u>ie</u>.

MEMORY LESSON #4: Create sentence cues for learning lists.
MEMORY LESSON #5: Create acronyms for learning lists.
MEMORY LESSON #6: Make up a mnemonic to remind you how to spell
tricky spots in words.

"Unlike a computer, which stores related facts separately, the brain strives constantly to make associations. . . . In short, we use the nets woven by past experience to capture new information." ~ Geoffrey Cowley & Anne Underwood

YOUR TURN AGAIN

DIRECTIONS: It's important to practice new skills so that, before long, you "own" them and can apply them automatically as needed.

A. Create a spelling mnemonic for these words; trouble spots are underlined.

1. shep<u>herd</u>: _____

2. mois<u>ten</u>: _____

3. pa<u>tie</u>nce: _____

4. n<u>eigh</u>bor: _____

5. <u>wei</u>rd: _____

B. Create an acronym for the following:

1. absent without leave: _____

2. self-contained underwater breathing apparatus: _____

3. radio detecting and ranging: _____

4. United Nations International Children's Emergency Fund: _____

C. Create an acronym for the scientific method outlined below. **Use the most important word in each step**:

1. State the problem.   _____
2. Gather information on the problem.   _____
3. Form a hypothesis.   _____
4. Perform experiments to test the hypothesis.   _____
5. Record and analyze data.   _____
6. State the conclusion.   _____

D. Create a sentence cue for the biological classification system below:

1. kingdom
2. phylum   _____
3. class
4. order   _____
5. family
6. genus
7. species

DRAWING COMPARISONS

DIRECTIONS: Compare your "remedies" with these, understanding that there is no one correct way. It's whatever works best for you—and whatever will carry over to all the memorizing you'll be called upon to do. Afterward, do some focused reviewing. A QUIZ is sure to follow!

A. Spelling mnemonics:

    1. shep<u>herd</u>: The shep<u>herd</u> was watching his <u>herd</u>.
    2. mois<u>ten</u>: Mois<u>ten</u> <u>ten</u> rags.
    3. pa<u>tie</u>nce: It takes pa<u>tie</u>nce to <u>tie</u> a <u>tie</u>.
    4. n<u>eigh</u>bor: I have <u>eight</u> n<u>eigh</u>bors.
    5. <u>we</u>ird: <u>We</u> are <u>we</u>ird.

B. Acronyms: (These are all well-known!)

    1. absent without leave: **AWOL**
    2. self-contained underwater breathing apparatus: **SCUBA**
    3. radio detecting and ranging: **RADAR**
    4. United Nations International Children's Emergency Fund: **UNICEF**

C. Scientific method acronym:

    1. State the PROBLEM: P
    2. Gather INFORMATION on the problem: I
    3. Form a HYPOTHESIS: H
    4. Perform EXPERIMENTS to test the hypothesis: E
    5. RECORD and analyze data: R
    6. State the CONCLUSION: C

D. Biological classification sentence cue:

    1. kingdom
    2. phylum
    3. class   **<u>King</u> <u>Ph</u>illip <u>c</u>alls <u>o</u>ld <u>f</u>ools <u>g</u>ood <u>s</u>ouls.**
    4. order
    5. family
    6. genus
    7. species

> "You can remember any new piece of information if it is associated with something you already know." ~ Jerry Lucas

QUIZZING

A. Spelling: (The words' definitions are provided.)
1. person who takes care of sheep: _____
2. to dampen: _____
3. willingness to put up with waiting, etc.: _____
4. one who lives nearby: _____
5. odd; strange: _____

B. What do these ACRONYMS stand for?
1. AWOL: _____
2. SCUBA: _____
3. RADAR: _____
4. UNICEF: _____

C. The Scientific Method:
1.
2.
3.
4.
5.
6.

D. The Biological Classification System:
1.
2.
3.
4.
5.
6.
7.

SCORING: 22/22 = 100%   18/22 = 81%
           21/22 = 95%   17/22 = 77%
           20/22 = 90%   16/22 = 72%
           19/22 = 86%   15/22 = Refocus &
                               review OUT LOUD!

My score: _____/22
My grade: _____%

"Owning your success makes you feel good about it.
And when you feel good, you're likely to do more of
the same." ~ Regena Thomashauer

JUST DO IT!!!

A PICTURE IS WORTH A THOUSAND WORDS!

TRY THIS: Read this abbreviated version of this Aesop fable, "The Fox and the Crow." As you read, close your eyes and create a mental picture of the story. Then draw a picture/cartoon of what you "saw."

The Fox and the Crow

One fine afternoon, a crow sat happily on a tree branch with a piece of cheese clutched firmly in his beak. Far below wandered a hungry fox searching the woods for food. Looking up, he spied the crow and thought, "With a bit of luck and trickery, that cheese will be mine!"

"Dear Crow," he crooned, "you are the loveliest bird I have ever seen. Why, you shine more brightly than the brightest stars. Is it possible that your voice is as beautiful as you are?"

Needless to say, the crow, listening to these grand compliments, fluttered his wings and began to sing. And, of course, as he did so, the cheese popped right out of his beak and fell straight into the fox's waiting mouth!

What did you see? _____

_____

Your Picture:

MEMORY LESSON #7: Create mental pictures of your readings. That's because the brain has this remarkable ability to create and hold onto images. When you look at something, an electric impulse reaches the brain's vision center, and the same thing happens when you use your "mind's eye."

A MIND'S EYE SCIENCE LESSON

DIRECTIONS: Now put your "mind's eye" to work as you read this passage from the text, *Science Connections*.

IGNEOUS ROCKS: Magma forms deep in the Earth where temperatures and pressures are high. Magma has a low density and sometimes rises to the Earth's surface. When magma flows onto the Earth's surface, it is called lava. When lava or magma cools and becomes solid, **igneous rocks** form. The type of igneous rock that forms is based on whether the molten material cools within the Earth or on its surface.

    Intrusive igneous rocks form when magma cools underground. Because the magma is insulated by the surrounding rock, it cools slowly. Slow cooling allows large mineral particles, or grains, to form. Thus, intrusive rocks have relatively coarse textures. Granite is an example.

    When lava cools quickly on the Earth's surface, **extrusive igneous rocks** form. Rapid cooling allows very little time for mineral grains to form. Rhyolite and basalt are extrusive igneous rocks. Two other examples of extrusive rocks are pumice and obsidian. These two rocks are called volcanic glass. Lava and other materials may build up cone-shaped mountains called volcanoes. Volcanoes and lava flows are also extrusive rock bodies. (Feather, pp. 202-203)

DURING YOUR READING, WHAT DID YOU SEE?

_____

_____

_____

> "We think in pictures. Don't see an elephant. Try not to. It's impossible."
> ~ Jerry Lucas

> "It is impossible to think without a mental picture." ~ Aristotle

On a separate sheet, draw what you saw.

A MEMORY TEST

"God gave us memory so that we might have roses in December." ~ J. M. Barrie

DIRECTIONS: It's time to put your new memory lessons to use. You have three minutes to memorize all the items pictured below—and you will! GO!

THE MEMORY TEST CONTINUES

DIRECTIONS: Here's your chance to jot down every item you can remember, engaging your memory and the techniques you relied on to learn them.

1. _____
2. _____
3. _____
4. _____
5. _____
6. _____
7. _____
8. _____
9. _____
10. _____

11. _____
12. _____
13. _____
14. _____
15. _____
16. _____
17. _____
18. _____
19. _____
20. _____

I CORRECTLY remembered _____ items = _____%

The memory technique(s) I used: _____

_____

_____

If I had it to do over, what, technique if any, would I change/add?

_____

"Picturing yourself reaching a lofty goal can inspire you to improve your current performance." ~ Peg Thoms, Ph.D.

MORE MEMORY FACTS AND TIPS

DIRECTIONS: Check them off, if you already know that you should . . .

☐ 1. Remember to write things down, because writing causes the brain to process information deeply and helps refine our thinking. It's an important learning tool.

☐ 2. Visualize the facts you're reading about by reducing the information to about six key items, noting and analyzing the relationship between them and forming a mental picture.

☐ 3. Improve your senses of sight and sound to improve your memory. One way is to go outside, listen carefully to all the faint sounds of the night and study the sky. This will increase your ability to pay attention and notice details, too.

☐ 4. Take advantage of the brain's ability to remember information set to music. Try clapping out the information or repeating it to the beat of a familiar tune.

☐ 5. Fill up on "brain food," such as fish, chicken, pork, eggs, whole wheat breads and cereals, peanuts, sweet potatoes, bell peppers, blueberries, strawberries, oranges, grapefruit, spinach, and broccoli. Take a multivitamin, too!

☐ 6. Eat some of the protein (meat, fish, poultry) on your plate before eating the carbohydrates (breads, pasta, white potatoes) for a mental boost.

☐ 7. Consciously relax all your muscles right before trying to learn something.

☐ 8. Get a good night's sleep as it helps the brain store the memory of whatever you've studied. Losing just two hours of sleep one night may impair your ability to remember the next day. In other words, sleep too little and risk forgetting!

☐ 9. Not be too anxious, nervous, or worried. It will interfere with your ability to learn and remember. Ever been too nervous during a test to do well?

☐ 10. Role play information under study as it enhances memory. In other words, act out all those revolving electrons, historic battles, ocean currents, whatever!

☐ 11. Exercise! Research suggests that a brisk, 45 minute walk, three times a week, can increase your ability to reason and make decisions. That's because exercise improves circulation, which, in turn, nourishes your brain.

☐ 12. Exercise your mind with word games, such as crossword & jigsaw puzzles, Scrabble, Boggle, Hangman, etc. A few mind games follow . . .

NOW YOU KNOW, SO NO EXCUSES!!!

WORD PLAY

DIRECTIONS: Did you know that you can make over 200 words just using the letters in the word TRANSPORTATION? Well, it's true, so start filling up the page and count your words—but remember you are limited to these 14 letters!

TRANSPORTATION

BRAIN TEASERS

GET READY TO EXERCISE YOUR MIND:

1. Why can't a man living in Winston-Salem, North Carolina, be buried west of the Mississippi River? _____

2. Some months have 30 days, some have 31. How many have 28? _____

3. I have in my hand two U.S. coins which total 55 cents in value. One is NOT a nickel. What are the two coins? _____

4. A farmer had 17 sheep. All but nine died. How many does he have left? _____

5. An electric train is going south. The wind is blowing westerly. Which way does the train's smoke go? _____

6. What kind of bank does not keep money? _____

7. What can get bigger but not heavier? _____

8. Study each set of numbers and then determine which number should appear next in the series:
   a. 9 10 12 15 19 24 _____   c. 11 14 17 20 23 26 _____
   b. 21 19 17 15 13 11 _____   d. 57 53 49 45 41 37 _____

9. After a heavy meal, the night watchman went to work. In the morning, he told his boss that he had dreamed that a saboteur had planted a bomb in the factory, and that he felt it was a warning. His boss promptly fired him. Why?

   _____

10. According to the U.S. Constitution, if the vice-president were to die, who would be president?

    _____

11. The same five letters, rearranged to make two different words, can complete the blanks below. Try it:
    "I had to fire that idiot!" explained the boss. "Our company _ _ _ _ _ someone a lot less _ _ _ _ _.

12. How do you split nine apples evenly between ten people if you only have one spoon?

    _____

KEEP EXERCISING!

13. You watched a marathon in which Sam was faster than Jack, Denise beat Jim but lost to Jack. Who came in last? _____

14. At one particular fruit stand where clear thinking does not always reign, an orange costs 18 cents, a pineapple costs 27 cents, and a grape costs 15 cents. Using the owner's same logic, how much would a mango cost?_____

_____

15. If you have only one match, and you enter a room in which there is a kerosene lamp, an oil burner, and a wood-burning stove, which would you light first?

_____

16. What has four legs in the morning, two in the afternoon, and three at night?

_____

17. What comes once in a minute, twice in a moment, and never in a thousand years?

_____

PLOTTING PENNIES

You'll need a partner to play this game that improves both problem solving and critical thinking. Try it.

1. Draw a tic-tac-toe grid.
2. Take three pennies and give three to your partner.
3. Line your three pennies face up along the top row.
4. Line your partner's pennies face down along the bottom row.
5. Taking turns, move one penny to an empty space in any direction—one space at a time. Jumping spaces is NOT allowed.
6. The goal: Move all your pennies to your partner's starting line.

> "Mental challenges . . . can stimulate the brain to produce new connections at probably any age—but especially when young." ~ Tom Friend

"A lot of what we term 'forgetting' is failure to pay attention in the first place." ~ James McGaugh

1. He's still living; 2. All months have 28 days; 3. A nickel & a 50 cent piece; 4. 9; 5. There's no smoke; 6. Blood bank; 7. A balloon; 8. a. 30, b. 9, c. 29, d. 33; 9. He'd slept on the job; 10. The president; 11. NEEDS/DENSE; 12. Make apple-sauce; 13. Jim; 14. 15 cents (3 cents per letter); 15. The match; 16. A person crawls on all fours, then walks on two legs, and finally needs a cane in old age; 17. The letter "W."

Part 8

TESTWISENESS
ACTIVITIES

TAKE A TEST DRIVE . . .

1. In the space provided, "brainstorm" the word *test*. In other words, record everything that comes to mind when you think about taking tests—the good, the bad, the indifferent. Be ready to share.

2. Rate yourself as a test-taker in each of your major subjects, with *1* representing your poorest showing and *5* your best:

English   _____

Reading   _____

Math   _____

Social Studies   _____

Science   _____

Health   _____

Foreign Language   _____

> "Intelligence is your ability to know your strengths and weaknesses and to capitalize on the strengths while compensating for the weaknesses."
> ~ unknown

_____   _____   *Your Average Test-Taking Rating:* _____

3. Did you give yourself the exact same rating in each of your subjects? Probably not. So how do you account for the variations in your performance? _____

_____

_____

4. Have you ever panicked before/during a test? If so, when & why?

_____

_____

_____

FOOD FOR THOUGHT

QUESTION: Who seems to care more about your academic success, you or your parent(s)? _____

WHY? _____

_____

---

motivation: *whatever gets you moving, either externally (bribes, grounding) or internally (willpower, goals, self-satisfaction)*

QUESTION: What motivates you to tackle homework and study for tests? Check off those that apply to you, add others, & be ready to share.

_____ competing with myself   _____ meeting technical school requirements
_____ self-respect   _____ meeting college requirements
_____ parental approval   _____ meeting career requirements
_____ bribery ($, gifts . . .)   _____ _____
_____ meeting sports requirements   _____ _____
_____ competing with other(s)   _____ _____
_____ avoiding summer school   _____ _____
_____ scholarship hopes   _____ _____

---

competition: *trying to win/gain what is wanted by others; rivalry*

self-confidence: *a belief in one's own ability, power, judgment, etc.*

self-esteem: *thinking well of oneself; self-respect*

REMEMBER: **"Self-doubt is a terrible enemy; never give into it."** ~ unknown

---

"Self-esteem cannot be handed to a child; it must be earned. . . . The most reliable path to self-esteem is for a kid to attempt a goal he or she believes is too hard, to work toward it and, finally, to either accomplish it—run the mile, finish the book, write the report—or to feel that a good try was made." ~ Melissa Fay Greene

AT A HIGH COST

WITH THESE DICTIONARY DEFINITIONS IN MIND,

Cheat: "to play or do business in a way that is not honest; to deceive or trick"

Plagiarize: "to act or take and use as one's own (the thoughts, writings, etc. of another), especially to take and use (a passage or plot, etc.) from the work of another writer"

BE HONEST AND CHECK OFF THE ITEMS THAT APPLY TO YOU:

- ☐ 1. I have never brought a "cheat sheet" to a test.
- ☐ 2. I have never copied from a neighbor's test.
- ☐ 3. I have never asked for test questions from a fellow student who already took it.
- ☐ 4. I have never copied information from a book cover/flap in a book report, essay, etc.
- ☐ 5. I have never copied information from the encyclopedia or a reference book in a research paper.
- ☐ 6. I have never copied a fellow student's homework.
- ☐ 7. I have never had a parent or friend do an assignment for me.

> **"I was determined that no one would outwork me."** ~ Bill Bradley

I checked off _____ items. Hopefully, your total is a resounding "7," but you're in good company if it's not. According to a USA TODAY poll (2/1/99) of top-ranking public school students, **80%** said they had cheated or plagiarized in school. In a more recent USA TODAY poll (12/20/00), **seven out of ten** admitted that they had cheated on at least one school exam last year. Plagiarizing, like cheating, marks you as someone who thinks everyone is smarter, more capable of learning, than you. Not the kind of advertising you need! And you'll eventually be caught, so keep on reading so you'll <u>never</u> be tempted to cheat on a test or plagiarize—not ever again!

ME AND TEST TAKING

CHECK OFF ONLY THOSE ITEMS THAT ARE TRUE FOR YOU:

☐ 1. I usually cram for tests.

☐ 2. I study for all tests the same way, whether objective or essay.

☐ 3. I don't usually sleep well the night before a big test.

☐ 4. I never study and then go to bed asking myself test questions.

☐ 5. I plunge right in as soon as I get a test, seldom looking over the whole thing before getting started.

☐ 6. On occasion, I've ignored the directions completely and gone directly to the questions.

☐ 7. On occasion, I've misread the directions, such as answering several essay questions instead of the one or two required.

☐ 8. Occasionally, I've run out of time on a test.

☐ 9. More than once, I've forgotten on a test what I know I studied the night before.

☐ 10. I usually panic on tests—butterflies, sweaty palms, and/or forgetting much of what I knew.

☐ 11. I sometimes panic if I can't answer the very first question.

☐ 12. Tests are no big deal to me, and I seldom prepare for them.

☐ 13. I want my parent(s) to be proud of me, but I just can't keep all that stuff in my head for a test.

☐ 14. I am seldom satisfied with my test grades.

☐ 15. My parents, at least once, have resorted to bribery. If I do well, they promise to buy me something, etc.

☐ 16. I've been grounded at least once because of low test grades.

If you checked off 3 or more items, you need a new plan—now! Read on to become more testwise and successful!

125

BEING OBJECTIVE

DIRECTIONS: Decide which statements are true and which are false.

____ 1. It's best to start answering questions right away, rather than scanning the entire test first.

____ 2. Test items should be answered in the order presented, regardless of how long it takes to arrive at an answer.

____ 3. Even if considerable time remains, it's wise not to check over answers, even those you're uncertain about. It's too confusing.

____ 4. If you're not sure about an answer, make a stab at it with a wild guess. It's better than leaving it blank.

____ 5. Directions just use up time; you can figure out what's called for just by looking at the test.

____ 6. When answering a multiple choice item, you should quickly read the question along with each of the choices.

____ 7. On standardized tests, it's smart to check and make sure you marked your answer in the correct space.

____ 8. As a general rule, choices containing such words as *always, only, never, all*, etc. are probably NOT CORRECT or FALSE. These and similar words are known as **specific determiners**.

____ 9. It's best to tackle items that seem easiest to you, saving more challenging ones until later.

____ 10. Sometimes information contained in one item may help you answer another.

____ 11. On multiple choice tests, it's sometimes possible to eliminate a choice because it is so far-fetched or unrelated.

____ 12. Grammatical cues in the questions, such as **a, an, was, were**, can be helpful in choosing the correct answer.

Your Score: ___/12

NOW, LET'S GET TESTWISE . . .

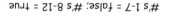
#'s 1-7 = false; #'s 8-12 = true

TEST PREP

"You don't start preparing for a test a couple of days before. You begin when you walk into the classroom that very first day. . . . Everything you do in a course—attending class, listening carefully, taking good notes, doing homework and assigned readings—helps you study for tests." ~ Ron Fry

BEFORE THE TEST: (Check off those items that are part of your test prep.)

☐ 1. Whatever you do, don't cram. Remember that memory curve!

☐ 2. Instead, find out test dates in advance & schedule weekly review sessions.

☐ 3. In addition to your textbook notes, be sure to use the two-column format when taking discussion and lecture notes by leaving a wide left-hand margin before beginning. Jot down all notes to the right of the fold; as soon as possible, add questions to accompany those notes to their left.

☐ 4. If you haven't already, make up flash cards for memorizing dates, vocab., etc.

☐ 5. Create acronyms, sentence cues, etc. to enhance learning and memory.

☐ 6. Create graphics based on major concepts. Find samples in the appendix.

☐ 7. Review by reciting from two-column notes; a number of those left-sided questions will likely appear in some form on the test.

☐ 8. Inquire as to the testing format: multiple choice, t/f, essay, etc. and make up questions to test yourself. Then check your text/notes to "grade" yourself.

☐ 9. If possible, ask your teacher to look over your self-made tests to make sure that you're targeting the important facts, concepts, details, etc.

☐ 10. Recite the questions and answers from your two-column notes/flash cards and take self-made tests as if you were in an actual testing situation. Set time limits, and with each review session, try to answer your questions more quickly.

☐ 11. Study by yourself initially. Once confident, it's fine to work with another.

☐ 12. Always ask questions in class when unclear about information.

☐ 13. Eat well and get plenty of sleep.

*Of these **13** items, I usually manage _____ when preparing for tests.*

Class average: _____ items

My Goal: Adding item #'s ____, ____, ____, ____, ____, ____, ____, ____, ____, ____

"Sorry, your ability to learn & retain new information is impaired by lack of REM sleep." ~ Louise Jarvis

BEING TESTWISE

DURING THE TEST: Check off those items that are part of your test-taking ritual.

- ☐ 1. Be well-prepared for confidence's sake. Confidence is half the battle!

- ☐ 2. Get to class quickly and give yourself a moment to unwind.

- ☐ 3. Have pencils/pen ready so you won't waste time getting organized.

- ☐ 4. Don't discuss the test at the last minute with friends. It will confuse you.

- ☐ 5. Listen carefully to and understand all directions before starting.

- ☐ 6. First, scan all directions & questions, planning your time according to the type, number, and difficulty of the questions while also establishing a mind-set.

- ☐ 7. Underline key words in the directions and follow them carefully.

- ☐ 8. Answer the easiest questions first but read all of them. This way, you will answer the ones you're sure of before time runs out, you may find an answer to another question, and you'll feel more confident.

- ☐ 9. Place a faint mark beside any questions you skip.

- ☐ 10. Time permitting, tackle skipped items, answering with *educated* guesses.

- ☐ 11. Don't leave any item unanswered. You know more than you think so make those educated guesses and fill in all blanks in the remaining minutes of the test.

- ☐ 12. Unless you guessed wildly, misread the question, or remembered something along the way, take care when changing answers. First responses are usually best.

- ☐ 13. Make sure your handwriting is legible.

- ☐ 14. Ignore other test-takers. The first done are not necessarily the smartest, plus they can be very unsettling.

> "Doing well on a test is a combination of knowing how to take a test and knowing the stuff that goes into the answers." ~ Ron Fry

Of these 14 items, I manage _____ during tests.

Class average: _____ items

My Goal: Adding item #'s ___, ___, ___, ___, ___, ___, ___, ___, ___, ___

THE REST OF THE STORY

What you do AFTER a test is as important as your preparation and performance. The old adage, "Learn from your mistakes," still rings true, so, on your next big test, take a coy of this with you and . . .

1. Remind yourself that you may have finished the test, BUT in the remaining time you must look it over, pretending you're the teacher with that proverbial red pen. Check to make sure that <u>all</u> items have been answered, that none has been misread or misinterpreted, and that careless mistakes will not jeopardize your grade.

2. Ask and answer such questions as:

   a. Now that I'm done, I think I did WELL/ JUST OKAY/REALLY BLEW IT (Circle one) because . . . _____
   _____
   _____

   b. The easiest thing about this test was . . . _____
   _____
   _____

   c. The hardest thing about this test was . . . _____
   _____
   _____

   d. In thinking about the test, I feel I was WELL-PREPARED/FAIRLY WELL-PRE-PARED/UNPREPARED (Circle one). From now on . . . _____
   _____
   _____

3. Study and correct all returned tests.
4. Talk with your teacher to understand where you went wrong on the test.

> "Everyone has what it takes to fail. To succeed is a far harder thing." ~ Edgar Degas

> *"If you care enough about a result, you will most certainly attain it." ~ William James*

IT TAKES TWO

DIRECTIONS: What do you already know about objective (matching, multiple choice, true/false) and essay tests? How do they differ, and what characteristics do they share? In the Venn Diagram below, note differences in the large circles; where the circles overlap, record the similarities between the two types of tests. You'll find details on the upcoming pages.

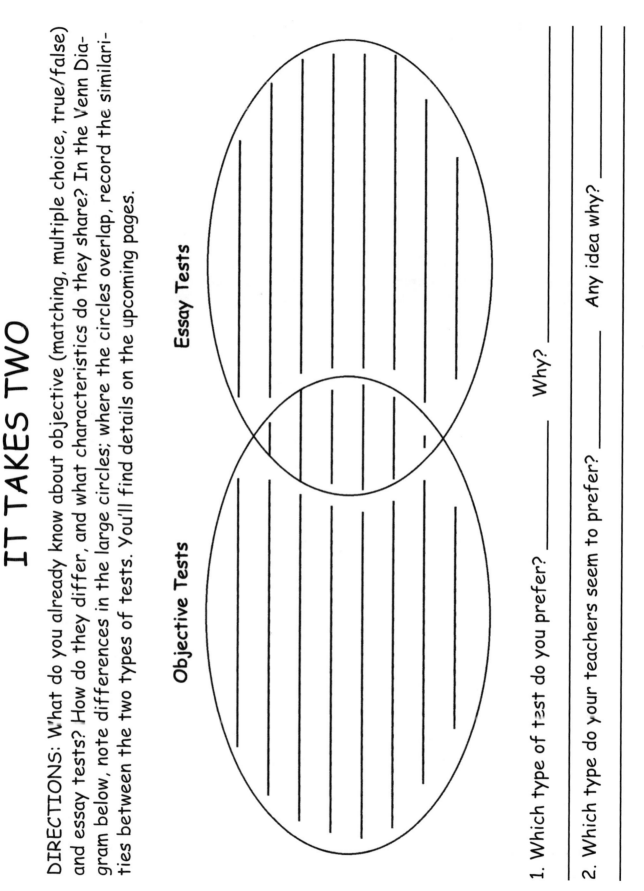

Objective Tests

Essay Tests

1. Which type of test do you prefer? _____ Why? _____

2. Which type do your teachers seem to prefer? _____ Any idea why? _____

_____

130

MULTIPLE CHOICE TEST TIPS

DIRECTIONS: Highlight "news to you" items. We'll make a note of them later.

1. **Stems** are statements to be completed/the question; **options** are your choices.

2. Underline key words, such as *not, except, false, correct, incorrect.* These words, if ignored, will trick you every time.

3. It's best to read the stem and then anticipate the answer before checking out all of the options. Even if you didn't anticipate the *exact* answer, you'll likely find an option that comes close.

4. Read and consider all of the options. Don't stop if/when you find the answer you anticipated. Sometimes more than one is correct, such as "both A & B are correct."

5. The key to multiple choice tests is eliminating options. If you eliminate just one option, your chances of being right improve by at least 20%. However, don't eliminate a choice unless you're certain.

6. Eliminate absurd (ridiculous) options immediately. For instance, if asked about the most popular American sports, you would promptly eliminate *gambling* because it's simply not a sport!

7. If two choices are very similar, they are either BOTH correct or incorrect.

   A <u>tale</u> is synonymous with:
   a. lyric
   b. fable
   c. legend
   d. both B & C are correct

   > Fable & legend are similar, so both are correct.

8. If two choices are opposites, both may be incorrect, but both can't be correct.

   The objective of the Women's Lib Movement was:
   a. to establish males as superior in America (somewhat absurd)
   b. to improve the American economy   (absurd)
   c. *total equality of the sexes*
   d. none of the above
   e. all of the above

(**a** & **c** are opposites, so eliminate **e**; **b** is absurd, so you're left with only two choices)

MORE MULTIPLE CHOICE TIPS

9. Treat each option as if it were a true/false item, keeping in mind that options with specific determiners (such as *always, never, every, all*) are <u>usually</u> false or incorrect. For instance:

    Choose the CORRECT answer among the following:
    a. Week after week, "West Wing" is *always* rated #1.
    b. "Frasier" is a remarkably popular TV comedy.
    c. *Every* teenager is hooked on MTV.
    d. *Nobody* ever watches "Murder She Wrote."

    Choose the INCORRECT answer among the following:
    a. Philadelphia has *never* experienced a hurricane.
    b. Philadelphia is known as the "City of Brotherly Love."
    c. Philadelphia's football team is the Eagles.
    d. Philadelphia is the nation's fifth largest city.

10. An option has a good chance of being correct if it contains such words as *usually, sometimes, probably, some*, etc., as in "Philadelphia *sometimes* experiences hurricanes."

11. Occasionally, you'll have to choose the BEST CHOICE from the options available to you. This does not necessarily mean that the best answer is completely true or false, just that it's the best of those offered. Find it through a process of elimination. For instance:

    Coffee, tea, and milk are:
    a. *beverages*
    b. stimulants
    c. liquids
    d. caffeinated drinks

    > It's true that they are all liquids, but that's not your best option, because *beverages* is a more specific response.

12. Eliminate the obvious or pretty obvious:

    The first US president to appoint a female to the Cabinet was:
    a. Abe Lincoln   (Women couldn't even vote then)
    b. *Franklin Roosevelt*   (Made sweeping changes)
    c. Herbert Hoover   (Made few, if any, major changes)
    d. George Bush   (Too recent to be the first)

13. When you don't know the right answer, look for the wrong ones.

EVEN MORE M.C. TIPS

14. Relate each option to the stem, asking yourself if it makes sense, is grammatically correct, etc. If not, eliminate that option. For instance:

    In the Garden of Eden, Eve offered Adam *an*
    a. plum   c. *apple (Only AN apple is grammatically correct)*
    b. kiwi   d. grape

15. Make sure that you read EVERY option. Your teacher may very well have placed a decoy option that is *almost* right, or seems so, tempting you to select it before you even look at the other choices.

16. When confronted by a long passage with questions to follow, read the questions FIRST. That way you'll know what to look for as you read—and it will affect the way you read. For example, if dates are asked for, you'll circle all of them in the passage. And remember, when answering, read the question and try to answer it before looking at the options. If your answer is one of them, bingo!

17. Quite often, the longest or most complicated option is the correct one. Your teacher had to include more information to make that answer complete.

18. When you see "all of the above" as one of your options, it's *often*, but not always, the correct one.

19. When you see "none of the above" as an option, you don't have to be positive that none are correct, just reasonably sure.

20. Place a faint mark next to questions that you leave blank or guessed at and go back to them if time permits after you've answered all the other questions.

21. Don't give up an a question that, at first, seems mind boggling. Instead, when you go back to it, look at it from a different angle. For instance, try restating it in your own words or even draw a picture of it, and you might just figure it out!

22. Time permitting, ** all items you were unsure of/guessed at, so when the test is returned, you'll know how your hunches panned out. Then check handouts, text, and lecture notes to see where those questions came from and why you missed them.

MAKE SURE YOU'VE HIGHLIGHTED ITEMS THAT ARE NEW TO YOU!

A NEW APPROACH

DIRECTIONS: Glance through all your highlighted multiple-choice tips. Then choose the most noteworthy among them and record them below. Remember that by writing them down you'll be more apt to keep them in mind for immediate implementation.

1. _____

   _____

2. _____

   _____

3. _____

   _____

4. _____

   _____

5. _____

   _____

6. _____

   _____

7. _____

   _____

8. _____

   _____

9. _____

   _____

10. _____

   _____

> "What can I do with what I've got? How I choose to respond makes all the difference." ~ Bob Wheelan

ON BEING TRUE OR FALSE

DIRECTIONS: Check off every unfamiliar tip.

☐ 1. If a test presents you with several types of questions, tackle the true/false ones first. They take the least amount of time to complete.

☐ 2. Tread carefully. True/false tests can be tricky, so know your stuff but also read each question carefully, critically. That doesn't mean reading more into a question; it just means be mindful and test-wise, paying attention to every word.

☐ 3. As on all tests, pace yourself and don't stall out on a puzzling question. Mark or skip troubling items and keep right on going.

☐ 4. As you proceed through the test, be mindful of possible clues along the way that may be helpful in answering other questions.

☐ 5. If you only *think* you know the answer, record it and don't change it. This is not a wild guess but a hunch based on what you've learned and the odds favor that you're right! And speaking of odds, don't forget that you have a 50-50 chance of being right on every true/false item in the first place!

☐ 6. Change an answer ONLY if you're *absolutely* sure you've made a mistake. Perhaps your memory was triggered by another question, or you discovered the right answer along the way. Just be sure! Haven't you at least once changed an answer only to discover you were right initially?

☐ 7. Questions containing specific determiners, such as *always, never, none,* and *all* are USUALLY false—but not ALWAYS. Few things ever are, and, anyway, it's hard to write a statement that is *always* true.

☐ 8. Also be on the alert for clue words that USUALLY make a statement true, such as *generally, sometimes,* and *usually.* (It's <u>false</u> that I am *always* happy, but if you say that I am *sometimes* happy, well, yes, that's most likely <u>true</u>.)

KEEP GOING . . .

135

MORE ON T/F TESTS

☐　9. Sometimes two parts of a statement are true, but the relationship between them makes them false. For instance: *Since Maine usually endures severe winters, the state is known for its potato farms and forests.* Understand that a cold winter does not necessarily cause its numerous potato farms and vast forests, so it's a false statement.

☐ 10. The hardest part about taking a true/false test is finding that one part is true—you're positive—but the other is definitely false. Don't be trapped. To be <u>true</u>, the whole thing must be true. Otherwise, your answer must be <u>false</u>.

☐ 11. The longer or more complicated a statement is, the more likely it is to be <u>false</u>. There are just too many chances for a single falsehood to slip in. All it takes is one small word or phrase to change an otherwise true statement into a false one. And remember: to be true, a statement must be entirely true.

☐ 12. Don't get tricked into thinking in patterns, such as, "This one must be false; there have been too many true ones in a row." So? There is no pattern. Just use your head and answer the questions!

☐ 13. Once done, if time permits, go back to those skipped items and answer them with educated—not wild—guesses.

YOUR TOP FIVE, BY ITEM #:

_____　_____　_____　_____　_____

WHAT YOU'VE LEARNED ABOUT T/F TESTS:

_____

_____

_____

_____

_____

THE MATCHING GAME

1. Items in Column 1 are the **stems**; those in Column 2 are the **options** or choices.

2. Read both lists carefully and completely, giving yourself an opportunity to find the obvious matches right away. Then tackle the rest one by one.

3. Fill in the blanks with CAPITAL, not lower case, letters, so there's no chance of being misread by your teacher.

4. When matching a word to a phrase, as on vocabulary tests, read the phrase first and then look for the word it describes in Column 1.

5. If stuck for an answer when matching one word to another, determine the part of speech of each word to help you. They should be the same.

6. If stuck for an answer when matching one word to another and the stem item is capitalized, then its match should be, too!

7. The position of the options in Column 2 can make a difference:

   a) On history tests, you often must match the names and events in Column 1 with dates and events in column 2. Realizing that you're unlikely to match an event with an event or a date with a name, your chances for success improve. That's because you'll be aiming to match first Column names with second Column events, and Column 1 events with Column 2 dates.

   b) Teachers usually don't place the correct option right across from its stem in Column 1. So, if you think you've got a side-by-side match-up, be sure to think twice.

8. DON'T count on it, but if Column 2 has more options than Column 1 has stems, it's possible that your teacher tagged them on at the last minute, not wanting the test to be too easy. Therefore, if you are left with an option in the middle and one at the end, that middle one is probably the better choice.

9. Cross out each answer as you find it—unless they can be used more than once.

10. As always, leave no blanks. Just make educated guesses as you finish up.

OF THESE 10 TIPS, I ALREADY DO _____ OF THEM.

ONE MORE MATCH-UP

Can you name three things a teacher can do to complicate a matching test?

1. _____

2. _____

3. _____

DIRECTIONS: Make up a matching test based on current studies and exchange with a fellow student. Make it fair, but use all those "tricks of the trade," providing plenty of practice. Later, grade & discuss.

___ 1.	a
___ 2.	b
___ 3.	c
___ 4.	d
___ 5.	e
___ 6.	f
___ 7.	g
___ 8.	h
___ 9.	i
___ 10.	j

Saying options can be used more than once; some not at all.
By adding, "None of the above" as an option.
Offering more options than questions.

TESTING, 1, 2, 3

DIRECTIONS: Here's a little testing workout designed with you in mind—at least your willingness to read each item carefully and critically, mindful of the many cues scattered throughout. Do so and ace it!

TRUE/FALSE: (10 points)

_____ 1. It's best to scan the entire test before starting to answer questions.

_____ 2. Test items should always be answered in the order presented.

_____ 3. Directions can be confusing, so definitely ignore them.

_____ 4. When in doubt, always guess blindly, leaving no blanks behind.

_____ 5. It's usually a good idea to answer the easiest questions first, and then go back and tackle the more difficult items.

_____ 6. Sometimes information contained in one item is helpful in another.

_____ 7. Never change an answer; go with your initial hunch.

_____ 8. Talk to friends before a test, so as to pick up last-minute information.

_____ 9. Anxiety is generally paralyzing, so relax and do your best.

_____ 10. True/false tests are always the hardest type of objective test.

MATCHING: (4 points)

_____ 11. specific determiner
_____ 12. options
_____ 13. absurd
_____ 14. stem

a. question
b. none
c. answers
d. seldom
e. ridiculous
f. generally
g. cue

MULTIPLE CHOICE: (6 points)

15. It's a good idea to find out test dates in advance, so that

    a. you can plan on being absent

    b. you can set up a study schedule

    c. you won't need to cram the night before

    d. it makes your teacher happy

    e. both B & C are correct

YOU'RE NOT DONE YET . . .

TESTING, 4, 5, 6

16. You should answer the easiest questions first, but try all of them because . . .
    a. you will have answered all those you're certain of before time runs out
    b. you may find the answer to one you're not sure of along the way
    c. you'll find that they are all easy & this will boost your confidence
    d. both A & B are correct
    e. none of the above is correct

17. You should place a faint mark beside skipped questions so . . .
    a. your teacher will know these were difficult for you and feel guilty
    b. you can add them up and know how many you'll get wrong beforehand
    c. you'll remember to go back to them
    d. you'll add them up and realize you should have studied harder
    e. both B & C are correct

18. Other test takers can . . .
    a. give you a sense of self-confidence
    b. help you pace yourself through test
    c. be useful when confronted by a question you're unsure of
    d. be unsettling
    e. none of the above

19. Grammatical cues can help you eliminate an option because . . .
    a. each option should agree grammatically with its stem
    b. your teacher wants you to do well
    c. they show that the test was poorly written
    d. none of the above

20. All of these are specific determiners, except . . .
    a. always
    b. never
    c. sometimes
    d. none
    e. every

Your Score: ____/20 = ____%
(Score below 80%? REVIEW!!!)

ONE VERSUS THE OTHER

Objective tests are tests of recognition. The answer is there in black and white—you just have to identify it, or know whether it is true or false. And many teachers prefer giving them. They may take a long time to create, but grading them is a snap! The answer is usually either right or wrong.

Essay tests, on the other hand, are tests of recall, requiring that you remember information and express yourself well in writing. Many teachers avoid this type of test, even though creating one takes only a short while. Grading them is the problem, not to mention the time it takes to do so! Essay tests also cause many students to shudder, but they really needn't.

THE ESSAY TEST ADVANTAGE

1. No tricks in the form of partially true statements, specific determiners, "none of the aboves," uneven matching lists, etc.

2. Here you have an opportunity to include all the information you have learned on a particular topic—not just the specifics targeted on an objective test.

3. You can even bluff a bit! After all, you've been listening in class, diligently taking notes . . .

4. You have time to sort out information and record it to your liking.

5. There's always the possibility of partial credit. It's unlikely that your response is completely wrong—unlike an objective test item.

THE ESSENTIALS

1. To be successful on an essay test, you must develop your writing skills.

2. You'll also have to organize all your ideas and facts in a coherent manner.

3. You must know the meanings of direction words, such as *compare* and *prove,* in order to proceed.

SO, LET'S BE ON OUR WAY. . .

DIRECTION WORD INVENTORY

DIRECTIONS: Match up the term with its appropriate definition.

_____ 1. COMPARE

_____ 2. DEFINE

_____ 3. DESCRIBE

_____ 4. EXPLAIN

_____ 5. JUSTIFY

_____ 6. SHOW

_____ 7. SUMMARIZE

_____ 8. LIST

_____ 9. CONTRAST

_____ 10. CRITICIZE

_____ 11. DISCUSS

_____ 12. PROVE

**(ANSWERS ARE ON
THE NEXT PAGE . . .)**

a. To emphasize differences, while perhaps mentioning similarities

b. the most general of all directions; to examine a topic in as much detail as time allows

c. to arrange in a numbered series

d. to present so as to be "seen"

e. to show to be right or reasonable; to give the reasons for something

f. to tell or write about in some detail

g. to make a short statement of the main points

h. to make clear or understandable

i. to state the exact meaning

j. to show similarities between two things

k. to examine & judge, presenting both the positive & negative points

l. to show to be true by giving facts and reasons

THOSE DIRECTION WORDS DEFINED

There's no way around it. In order to respond to an essay question, you must know the meaning of its direction word. Otherwise you're lost.

- COMPARE   to show similarities between things

- CONTRAST   to emphasize differences, while similarities might be mentioned

- CRITICIZE   to examine & judge, presenting both negative and positive aspects

- DEFINE   to state the exact meaning(s)

- DESCRIBE   to write about in some detail (similar to *discuss*)

- DISCUSS   the most general of all directions; to examine a topic in as much detail as time allows

- EXPLAIN   to make clear or understandable

- JUSTIFY   to show to be right or reasonable; to give the reasons for something

- LIST   to arrange in a numbered series

- PROVE   to show to be true by giving facts and reasons

- SHOW   to present so as to be "seen"

- SUMMARIZE   to make a short statement of the main points

YOUR SCORE: ____/12   *NOW, MAKE THOSE FLASH CARDS!*

THE ART OF ESSAYING

If you think the key to essay writing is quickly writing down everything about a topic that comes to mind, you're wrong. And if you think your teacher will be impressed by pages of thoughtless writing, you're wrong again. We're aiming for quality, not quantity, so follow these tips to be a more successful essayist. ***Highlight whatever is new to you.***

1. Make sure you are well-prepared, having tested yourself with some self-made essay questions as part of your study regime.
2. Don't begin until you've listened carefully to your teacher's instructions, knowing beforehand . . .
   a. Whether you have the full period to work
   b. Whether *all* questions must be answered, or if there is a choice
   c. If all the questions are worth the same number of points
   d. If you are allowed to use a dictionary and/or thesaurus
   e. Whether any corrections or additions need to be made to the test
3. Read *all* questions carefully.
4. Pay careful attention to direction words, so you'll know HOW to answer.
5. If you have any questions, ask them right away before everyone begins.
6. Once you begin, pace yourself, keeping in mind how much time you can allot to each question, and stick to your schedule or risk running out of time.
7. Don't spend so much time on one question that you can't devote enough time to the other(s).
8. Think before you write, outlining or mapping your main ideas and facts. Then add specific details and examples.
9. Order your notations so that one leads logically to the next in your essay.
10. Rewrite the question as your introductory statement. For example, if asked to describe terrible conditions for George Washington and his men at Valley Forge, you might start by writing, "Conditions were terrible for George Washington and his soldiers camped at Valley Forge."
11. If possible, rev up your lead sentence, immediately grabbing your instructor's attention. For instance: "Do you think you could sit outside in snowy temperatures hovering around the ten degree mark? Washington and his crew did at Valley Forge that awful winter of 1777-78." (Jason Davis, 8th grade)
12. Stick to your topic and don't include unrelated information.
13. If unsure how to answer a remaining question, just start writing. You'll seldom be asked a question you know nothing about.
14. Write legibly, stick to the margins, and always proofread.
15. Use returned essay tests to determine weaknesses, so you'll improve.

PRACTICE LEADING

DIRECTIONS: Here are some lead sentences written by middle-schoolers. Read and think about them carefully. Do they catch your attention?

TOPIC: **The German invasion of Poland which triggered WWII:**
   A loud roar echoed throughout the Polish countryside, the clear blue sky quickly turning black with billowing clouds of smoke. (Kelly Ballady)

TOPIC: **Madame Curie:**
   She received the Nobel Prize in chemistry for her discovery of radium and polonium, but France's Academy of Science refused to grant Madame Curie membership because she was a woman. (Terrell Muchison)

TOPIC: **Joe Frazier:**
   In 1944, one of the best heavyweight fighters was born. (Patrick O'Brien)

TOPIC: **George Washington's Christmas crossing of the Delaware River:**
   All you could hear was the paddle hitting the water and the hoot of an owl.
                                                                    (Jennifer Kohern)

Now it's your turn to write a great lead. Here are your facts:

◆ Roaches have been around for 350 million years, predating the dinosaur.
◆ Young roaches, called nymphs, will molt and grow a new skeleton six to twelve times before reaching adulthood. Should a nymph lose an appendage during that process, no problem. It will grow a new one the next time it molts.
◆ Roaches can eat almost anything—even cancer-causing poisons—and survive.
◆ The American roach migrated here from Africa aboard slave ships.
◆ The Danish navy rewarded sailors with a flask of brandy for every 1,000 roaches they killed. The greatest catch on a single ship was 32,000 roaches.
◆ If a roach were the size of a human being, it could run up to 90 miles per hour.

Your Lead Sentence: _____

_____

Revise/edit and make it even better: _____

_____

DID YOU KNOW THAT. . .

- In 1895, King C. Gillette invented the first safety razor with disposable blades?
- In 1905, Orville Wright completed his first 30 minute flight?
- In 1906, the San Francisco earthquake leveled 490 city blocks?
- In 1909, Commander Robert E. Perry planted the U.S. flag in the North Pole?
- Also in 1909, Henry Ford began assembly line production of motor cars?
- In 1910, the Boy Scouts of America was chartered by William Boyce?
- In 1912, the Girl Scouts of America held its first meeting as the Girl Guides?
- Also in 1912, the *Titanic* struck an iceberg and sank?
- In 1922, King Tut's tomb was found and opened in Egypt?
- Also in 1922, the Lincoln Memorial was dedicated after seven years of construction?
- In 1927, Charles A. Lindbergh, in the *Spirit of St. Louis,* made the first nonstop solo flight between New York's Roosevelt Field to Paris, France?
- In 1929, the stock market crashed on October 24th?
- In 1934, a rocky mountain in San Francisco Bay became a maximum security prison called Alcatraz?
- In 1944, 176,000 troops stormed the beaches of Normandy on June 6th, under the command of Dwight D. Eisenhower?
- In 1945, atomic bombs were dropped on Japan's Hiroshima and Nagasaki?

NOW, choose three of the above events you find most interesting:

1. _____

2. _____

3. _____

GO SEARCHING

DIRECTIONS: Go back to your three selections on the previous page and star your favorite. Then it's off to the library to research and discover some facts/details about your topic, all the while asking yourself such questions as.

1. When exactly did it happen?
2. Where did it happen?
3. Why did it happen?
4. How did it happen?
5. What caused it?
6. Who was involved?
7. It was preceded by?
8. It was followed by?
9. What were its results or effects?

Fill in these blanks with your facts as you do your research.

_____

_____

_____

_____

_____

_____

_____

_____

_____

_____

_____

IN THE LEAD

DIRECTIONS: Once a leading, introductory sentence is written, you still have to devise the rest of your opening paragraph. Here's a sample:

TOPIC: *Florenz Ziegfield*

      Would you carry your clothes and toothbrush rolled up in a newspaper whenever you traveled? Well, that's what Ziegfield of the Ziegfield Follies did—not because he couldn't afford a suitcase but because he simply wanted to.

(Carol Pagnotti)

Your Topic: _____

Most important facts from previous page:

- ◆ _____
- ◆ _____
- ◆ _____
- ◆ _____
- ◆ _____
- ◆ _____

Your introductory lead sentence and first paragraph: _____

_____

_____

_____

_____

_____

_____

_____

_____

Revise/edit and write your well-polished introductory paragraph on a separate sheet of paper and be prepared to share what you've learned.

WHAT YOUR TEACHER LOOKS FOR (AND SO SHOULD YOU!)

1. Is there a strong introductory sentence?

2. Is there a satisfying conclusion?

3. Is the response in keeping with the direction word?

4. Are all major points covered?

5. Is the essay logically organized?

6. Are all the sentences in a paragraph related to its main idea?

7. Were all parts of the question answered?

8. Is the essay correctly punctuated?

9. Is the essay grammatically correct?

10. Are all words spelled correctly?

11. Is the handwriting readable?

12. Is there evidence of proofreading?

MISTAKES TO LEARN FROM

DIRECTIONS: Think carefully about some recent tests you've taken, check off the answers that apply, and learn from your mistakes.

PREPPING:

☐ 1. I didn't take two-column notes on my textbook or handouts.
☐ 2. I didn't recite, instead I studied silently.
☐ 3. I left my studying for the night before.
☐ 4. I forgot to make a note of when the test would be—and forgot about it.
☐ 5. I did all my studying with a friend.
☐ 6. I stayed up way too late and/or skipped breakfast.

TEST-TAKING:

☐ 1. I knew the right answer but wrote/circled the wrong letter/number.
☐ 2. I didn't look over the whole test initially, so I didn't realize there were more questions on the back.
☐ 3. I didn't figure out how much time I could spend on each item, and I ran out of time.
☐ 4. I misread the directions, such as "Which answer is NOT correct."
☐ 5. I didn't outline and order my essay beforehand and got off the topic as I wrote.
☐ 6. I ignored such words as *always, never,* and *none,* marking a statement true when it was false or not correct.
☐ 7. I didn't make a mark next to skipped items, so I forgot to go back to one or two.
☐ 8. I changed one of my answers when I was right in the first place.
☐ 9. I ignored all the grammatical cues and answered incorrectly.
☐ 10. I forgot that if only part of the statement is true, then the answer has to be false.
☐ 11. I didn't know the meaning of one of the direction words.
☐ 12. I rushed because everyone was finishing before me, and I didn't want to be the last one done.

TO END, LET'S MAKE A FEW MORE PROMISES . . .

ONCE OVER LIGHTLY

A. Review ALL test-taking materials, both objective and essay.

B. Jot down five tips you didn't know before:

1. _____
2. _____
3. _____
4. _____
5. _____

C. Jot down five tips you knew already but tend to forget or ignore:

1. _____
2. _____
3. _____
4. _____
5. _____

D. Promised changes in the way to approach your studies and tests:

1. _____
2. _____
3. _____
4. _____
5. _____
6. _____
7. _____
8. _____
9. _____
10. _____

"You won't get good grades unless you work for them." ~ Carol's mother

APPENDIX

	Sat	Fri	Thu	Wed	Tue	Mon	Sun

The Pretty Good Student
By Charles Osgood

There once was a pretty good student who sat in a pretty good class and
Was taught by a pretty good teacher who always let pretty good pass.
He wasn't terrific at reading; he wasn't a whiz bang at math,
But for him, education was leading down a pretty good path.
He didn't find school too exciting, but he wanted to do pretty well.
He did have trouble with reading, and nobody taught him to spell.
In doing arithmetic problems, pretty good was regarded as fine.
Five and five needn't always add to ten; a pretty good answer was nine.
The pretty good student was happy with the standards that were in effect,
And nobody thought it was sappy if his answers were not quite correct.
The pretty good class he sat in was part of a pretty good school,
And the student was not the exception; on the contrary, he was the rule.
The pretty good student was, in fact, part of a pretty good mob.
The first time he knew what he lacked was when he looked for a pretty
   good job.
It was then when he saw that position, he discovered that life could be
   tough,
And he soon had a sneaking suspicion that pretty good might not be good
   enough.
The pretty good town in the story was part of a pretty good state,
Which had pretty good aspirations and prayed for a pretty good fate.
There once was a pretty good nation, pretty proud of the greatness it had,
But which learned much too late, if you want to be great,
Pretty good is, in fact, pretty bad.

We learn . . . .

10% of what we read,
20% of what we hear,
30% of what we see,
50% of what we both see and hear,
70% of what is discussed with others,
80% of what we experience personally,
95% of what we teach to someone else.

~ William Glasser

K-W-L

What do I already *know* about this subject?	What do I *want* to learn about this subject?	What have I now *learned* about this subject?

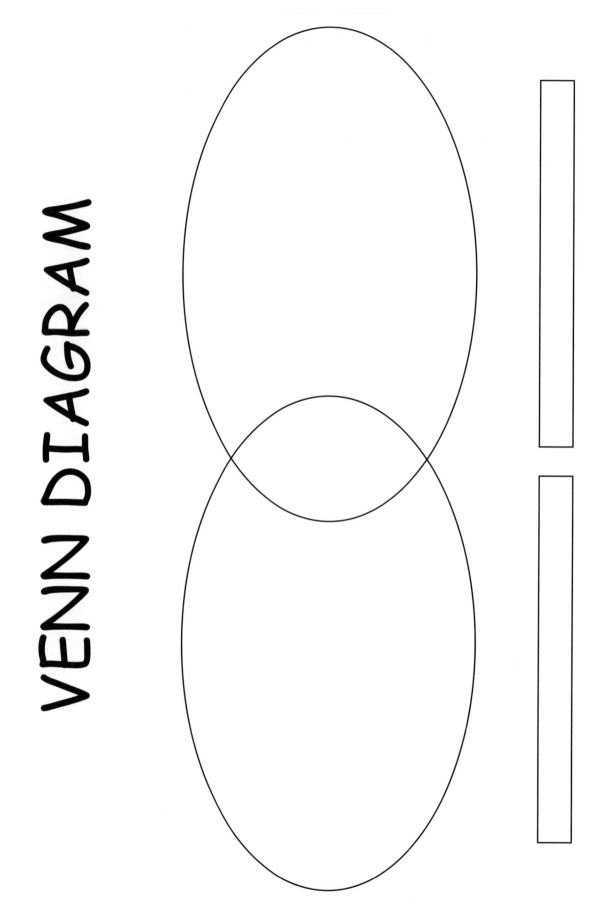

VENN DIAGRAM

T-CHART

(CAUSE-EFFECT, PROBLEM-SOLUTION, THEN-NOW, etc.)

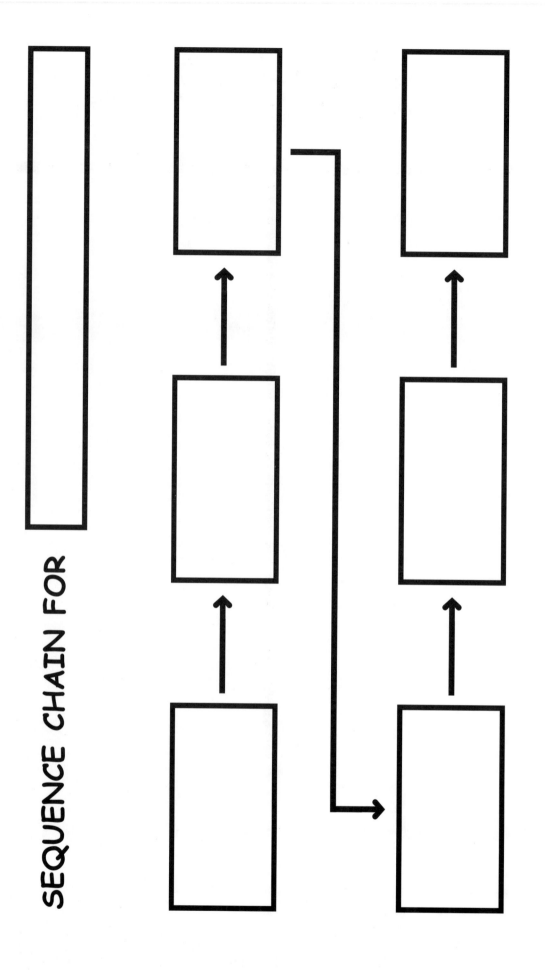

SEQUENCE CHAIN FOR

CONCEPT MAP

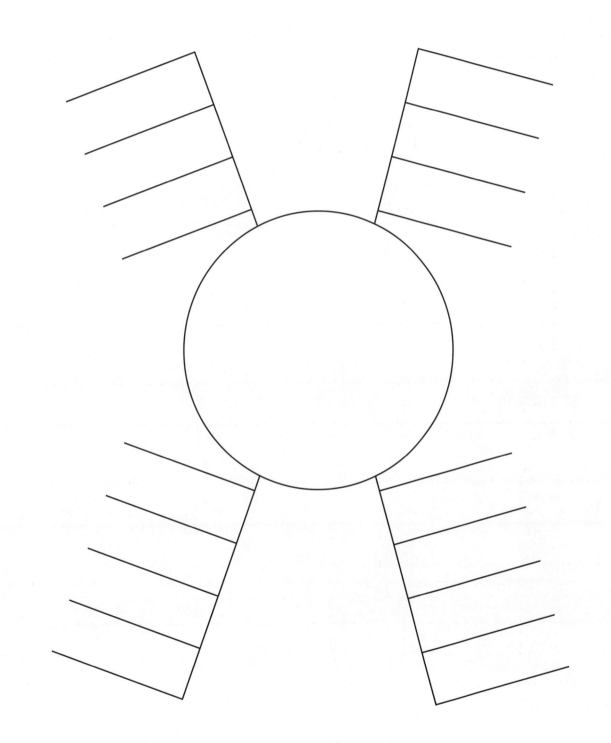

MAIN IDEA GRAPHIC

MAIN IDEA:_____

_____

DETAILS

FRAYER MODEL

ESSENTIAL CHARACTERISTICS

NON-ESSENTIAL CHARACTERISTICS

EXAMPLES

NON-EXAMPLES

163

USA SNAPSHOTS®

A look at statistics that shape the nation

Education and pay

Average 1998[1] earnings, based on educational level, for people 18 or older:

No high school diploma	$16,124
High school diploma	$22,895
Some college, no degree	$24,804
Associate degree	$29,872
Bachelor's degree	$40,478
Master's degree	$51,183
Doctoral degree	$77,445
Professional degree	$95,148

1– Most recent data available

Source: Census Bureau; *Current Population Reports*, March 1998

By James Abundis and Quin Tian, USA TODAY

January 6, 2000

USA SNAPSHOTS®

A look at statistics that shape the nation

Epidemic of cheating

Among teens who rank at the top of their classes, 80% say they've cheated (copied, plagiarized, etc.) in school. How common cheating is at these schools, say teens:

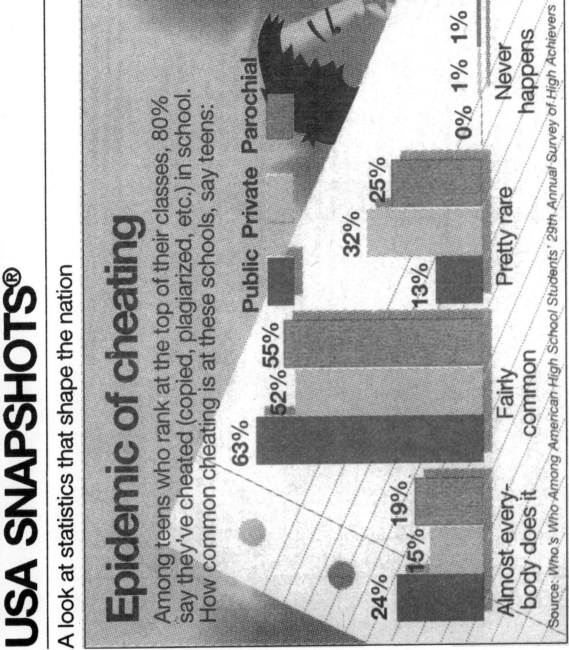

Public   Private   Parochial

63%	52% 55%	
		32%
	13%	25%
24%		
15% 19%		0% 1% 1%

Almost every-body does it

Fairly common

Pretty rare

Never happens

Source: *Who's Who Among American High School Students' 29th Annual Survey of High Achievers*

By Anne R. Carey and Sam Ward, USA TODAY

2/1/99

TAKE ACTION!!!

Like a promise to yourself, your action plan should reflect your intention to take charge of your student life and improve your attitude and/or approach to school-related tasks. Take aim at one area that needs immediate attention, jot down the steps required in order to make improvement a reality, and then get moving on them!

1. _____

2. _____

3. _____

4. _____

5. _____

7. _____

8. _____

9. _____

READING LOG

Date	Title/Author	Comments	# of pages

GRADE RECORD SHEET

Subject: _____

Marking Period: _____

Date	Homework, Quizzes, Tests, Projects, Reports	Pts. Possible	Pts. Earned

Bacon, John. "Author Sues over Harry Potter Ideas." *USA Today* 17 March 2000, D1. (see Muhammad below)

Begley, Sharon. "Music on the Mind." *Newsweek* (24 July 2000): 50–52.

——. "The Stereotype Trap." *Newsweek* (6 November 2000): 66–68.

Benjamin, Caren. "Want to Be Smarter, Longer?" *SELF* Magazine (May 2000): 101–103.

Bergonzi, Chris. "On the Brain." *The Walking Magazine* (September/October 2000): 138–39ff.

Bolster, L. Carey, et al. *Exploring Mathematics.* Glenview, Ill.: Scott, Foresman, and Company, 1991.

Chafetz, Michael D. *Smart for Life: How to Improve Your Brain Power at Any Age.* New York: Penguin, 1992.

Chase, Robert. "Tests and Sensibility." *National Education Association Today* (February 2000): 5.

Colligan, Louise. *Scholastic's A+ Guide to Taking Tests.* New York: Scholastic, 1982.

Cowley, Geoffrey, and Anne Underwood. "Memory." *Newsweek* (15 June 1998): 48–54.

Dionne, E. J. "Biden Faced Plagiarism Charges in Law School." *The Morning Call* 17 September 1987, A1–A2.

Ernst, John. *Middle School Study Skills.* Westminster, Calif.: Teacher Created Materials, 1996.

Fackelmann, Kathleen. "Deep Sleep Beats All-Nighter for Retaining What You Learn." *USA Today* 27 November 2000, D10.

Feather, Ralph M., et al. *Science Connections.* Columbus, Ohio: Merrill, 1990.

Flemming, Laraine E. *Reading for Results.* Boston: Houghton Mifflin, 1978.

Flippo, Rona. *Testwise: Strategies for Success in Taking Tests.* Belmont, Calif.: Fearon Teacher Aids, 1988.

Fry, Ron. *"Ace" Any Test.* Franklin Lakes, N.J.: Career, 1996.

——. *How to Study.* Franklin Lakes, N.J.: Career, 1991.

——. *Take Notes.* Franklin Lakes, N.J.: Career, 1991.

Gay, Greg. "Learning Styles Links." *Learning to Learn.* Adaptive Technology Resource Centre. snow.utoronto.ca/Learn2/resources/stylelinks.html, 12 October 1999 [accessed 9 December 2001].

Goldshlag, Patricia, et al. *Many Americans—One Nation.* New York: Noble and Noble, 1974.

Gordon, Sondra. "Could You Drink 597 Cans of Soda?" *SELF* Magazine (November 2000): 93.

Graff, Henry F. *The Free and the Brave: The Story of the American People.* Chicago: Rand McNally, 1980.

Graham, Kenneth G., and H. Alan Robinson. *Study Skills Handbook: A Guide for All Teachers.* Newark, Del.: International Reading Association, 1985.

Greenblatt, Miriam, and Peter S. Lemmo. *Human Heritage: A World History.* Columbus, Ohio: Merrill, 1989.

Hampson, Rick. "Sky's Dark Wall of Death Leaves Nowhere to Run." *USA Today* 20 December 2000, A1–A2.

Healy, Michelle. "Humor Has a Home in the Brain." *USA Today* 28 November 2000, D10.

Herber, Harold L. *Teaching Reading in the Content Areas.* Englewood Cliffs, N.J.: Prentice-Hall, 1978.

Hirsh, Stephanie A., and Phillip Bacon. *The United States: Its History and Neighbors.* Orlando, Fla.: Harcourt Brace Jovanovich, 1988.

Jones, Charisse. "Sudan's 'Lost Boys' Find New Homes, Live Across the USA." *USA Today* 20 December 2000, A1–A2.

Lane, Barry. *After the End: Teaching and Learning Creative Revision.* Portsmouth, N.H.: Heinemann, 1993.

Langan, John. *Reading and Study Skills.* New York: McGraw-Hill, 1982.

Larayne, Harry, and Jerry Lucas. *The Memory Book.* New York: Ballantine Books, 1974.

"Learning Styles Evaluation." *Learning Lab.* University of Northwestern Ohio. www2.nc.edu/virtcol/ss/learn.html, 1998 [acccessed 9 December 2001].

Mangrum, Charles T., et al. *Teaching Study Skills and Strategies in Grades 4–8.* Boston: Allyn & Bacon, 1998.

Michaud, Ellen, et al. *Boost Your Brain Power.* New York: MJF, 1991.

Mueser, Annie. *Using Textbooks Successfully.* New York: Scholastic, 1981.

Muhammad, Lawrence. "Experts Brainstorming Over Memory Loss." *USA Today* 30 March 1999, D1.

Page, Susan. "George W. Bush Takes Charge in Washington." *USA Today* 19–21 January 2001, A1–A2.

Pool, Lawrence. *Nature's Masterpiece: The Brain and How It Works.* New York: Walker and Company, 1987.

Savacool, Julia. "Can You See Success from Here?" *SELF* Magazine (December 2000): 101.

Sebranek, Patrick. *Write Source 2000: A Guide to Writing, Thinking, & Learning.* Wilmington, Mass.: Great Source Education Group/Houghton Mifflin, 1995.

Sorgen, Marny, and Pat Wolfe. *Strengthening Student Learning by Applying the Latest Research to Your Classroom Teaching.* Bellevue, Wash.: Bureau of Education and Research, 1994.

Soriano, Cesar G. "Supreme Court Rejects Bolton's Appeal." *USA Today* 23 January 2001, D1.

Thorndike, E. L. *Scott, Foresman Intermediate Dictionary.* Glenview, Ill.: Scott, Foresman and Company, 1979.

Tierney, Robert J., et al. *Reading Strategies and Practice: A Guide for Improving Instruction.* Boston: Allyn and Bacon, 1980.

"With Toys Like This, Who Needs Friends?" *Newsweek* (13 November 2000): 14.

Carol Josel, a graduate of the University of Maine (B.A. English/French), holds a master's of education degree in reading with supervisory and principal certification from Beaver College. A teacher since 1966, she is currently a learning specialist with the Methacton school district in Pennsylvania, working with middle school-aged children and their parents. She is also the author of *Ready-to-Use ESL Activities for Every Month of the School Year* (Center for Applied Research in Education), and her writings have appeared in such professional publications as *Teaching Pre-K–8* and *The Journal of Adolescent and Adult Literacy*.